Universal Compassion

Also by Geshe Kelsang Gyatso

Meaningful to Behold
Clear Light of Bliss
Buddhism in the Tibetan Tradition
Heart of Wisdom
The Meditation Handbook
Joyful Path of Good Fortune
Guide to Dakini Land
The Bodhisattva Vow
Heart Jewel
Great Treasury of Merit
Introduction to Buddhism
Understanding the Mind
Tantric Grounds and Paths
Ocean of Nectar

Universal Compassion

TRANSFORMING YOUR LIFE THROUGH LOVE AND COMPASSION

GESHE KELSANG GYATSO

MOTILAL BANARSIDASS PUBLISHERS
PRIVATE LIMITED • DELHI

First Indian Edition : Delhi, 2002
First Published : U.K., 1988

In association with Tharpa Publications,
15 Bendemeer Road, London SW15 1JX

ISBN: 81-208-1868-7

Also available at:
MOTILAL BANARSIDASS
41 U.A. Bungalow Road, Jawahar Nagar, Delhi 110 007
8 Mahalaxmi Chambers, 22 Bhulabhai Desai Road, Mumbai 400 026
236, 9th Main III Block, Jayanagar, Bangalore 560 011
120 Royapettah High Road, Mylapore, Chennai 600 004
Sanas Plaza, 1302 Baji Rao Road, Pune 411 002
8 Camac Street, Kolkata 700 017
Ashok Rajpath, Patna 800 004
Chowk, Varanasi 221 001

Line illustrations by Andy Weber

British Library Cataloguing in Publication Data
A catalogue record for this book is available from the British Library

FOR SALE IN SOUTH ASIA ONLY

Printed in India
BY JAINENDRA PRAKASH JAIN AT SHRI JAINENDRA PRESS,
A-45 NARAINA, PHASE-I, NEW DELHI 110 028
AND PUBLISHED BY NARENDRA PRAKASH JAIN FOR
MOTILAL BANARSIDASS PUBLISHERS PRIVATE LIMITED,
BUNGALOW ROAD, DELHI 110 007

Contents

Illustrations

Acknowledgements

Universal Compassion is based on two courses of teachings given by Venerable Geshe Kelsang Gyatso at Manjushri Centre as commentaries to the celebrated root text *Training the Mind in Seven Points*, an important Mahayana Buddhist scripture written by the great Bodhisattva, Geshe Chekhawa (1102–1176). Inexpressible gratitude is due to Geshe Kelsang, first for the inspired oral commentaries upon which the book is based, and then for his supervision of every stage of the editing process, all carried out with immeasurable wisdom, patience, and kindness. Geshe Kelsang's great good qualities throughout acted as the mainspring of the entire endeavour, and we are confident that *Universal Compassion* will benefit many people. Such benefit is the sole intention of this great Teacher's every action.

We would also like to thank all the students of the author who, with great skill and dedication, edited the book and prepared it for publication.

Roy Tyson,
Administrative Director,
Manjushri Mahayana
Buddhist Centre,
November 1992

Editorial Note

Universal Compassion is a commentary to a twelfth-century text on training the mind entitled *Training the Mind in Seven Points,* which was composed by the great Tibetan Bodhisattva, Geshe Chekhawa. Throughout the book the lines from this root text are given in bold. The root text is also presented in full in Appendix I. It is hoped that the serious practitioner will memorize the root text, together with the condensed meaning of the commentary, which can be found in Appendix III.

Preface

Every living being has the same basic wish – to be happy and to avoid suffering. Even newborn babies, animals, and insects have this wish. It has been our main wish since beginningless time and it is with us all the time, even during our sleep. We spend our whole life working hard to fulfil this wish.

Since this world evolved, human beings have spent much time and energy improving external conditions in their search for happiness and a solution to their many problems. What has been the result? Instead of their wishes being fulfilled, human suffering has continued to increase while the experience of happiness and peace is decreasing. This clearly shows that we need to find a true method for gaining pure happiness and freedom from misery.

All our problems and all our unhappiness are created by our uncontrolled mind and our non-virtuous actions. By engaging in the practice of Dharma we can learn to pacify and control our mind, abandon non-virtuous actions and their root cause, and thereby attain permanent peace, the true cessation of all our suffering.

The supreme Dharma of training the mind (Tib. Lojong) is an unsurpassed method for controlling our mind, and reveals the principal path to enlightenment. There are many different sets of Lojong instructions such as those contained in the *One Hundred Practices of Training the Mind*. The present text, *Universal Compassion*, explains how to put into practice the Lojong instructions given by Bodhisattva Geshe Chekhawa in his root text *Training the Mind in Seven Points*. The seven points are:

1 The preliminary practices of training the mind
2 The main practice: training in the two bodhichittas
3 Transforming adverse conditions into the path to enlightenment
4 How to integrate all our daily practices
5 The measurement of success in training the mind
6 The commitments of training the mind
7 The precepts of training the mind

The first point, the preliminary practices, is the preparation for engaging in the principal path to enlightenment, and the second point is the principal path itself. The five remaining points are the methods for completing the principal path.

To have the opportunity to practise this precious and profound teaching is infinitely more meaningful than being given all the precious jewels in the world. If we understand how extremely worthwhile it is to read, listen to, study, contemplate, and engage in the practice of this very special Dharma, we shall do so with great faith and a happy mind.

Geshe Kelsang Gyatso,
Tharpaland,
November 1987

The Lineage and Qualities of Training the Mind

THE LINEAGE AND PRE-EMINENT QUALITIES OF THESE INSTRUCTIONS

The instructions on training the mind were originally given by Buddha Shakyamuni. He passed them to Manjushri, who transmitted them to Shantideva. From Shantideva they passed in unbroken succession to Elladari, Viravajra, Ratnashri, Serlingpa, Atisha, Dromtönpa, Geshe Potowa, Geshe Sharawa, and Geshe Chekhawa. Geshe Chekhawa composed the text *Training the Mind in Seven Points* and spread the study and practice of training the mind throughout Tibet. He transmitted the instructions to the Bodhisattva Chilbuwa and from him they passed through a succession of realized Masters to Je Tsongkhapa.

Several versions of the root text, *Training the Mind in Seven Points*, were compiled from notes taken by Geshe Chekhawa's disciples. Later, Je Tsongkhapa gave teachings on *Training the Mind in Seven Points* and, without contradicting other sources, clarified the meaning of these instructions according to the view and intentions of Geshe Chekhawa and Atisha. The notes of Je Tsongkhapa's disciples were collected into a text, known as *Sunrays of Training the Mind*, which is regarded as one of the most authoritative commentaries on training the mind. The version of the root text used in this book is the one compiled by Je Phabongkhapa, based on *Sunrays of Training the Mind*, *Essence of Nectar of Training the Mind*, and other texts. Thus, from Je Tsongkhapa the instructions on training the mind have come down in an unbroken lineage to present-day Teachers.

Buddha Shakyamuni

Homage to great compassion.
This essence of nectar-like instruction
Is transmitted from Serlingpa.

Geshe Chekhawa begins the root text by paying homage to great compassion. His purpose is to show that because all Buddhas and Bodhisattvas are born from the mother, great compassion, anyone wishing to become a Buddha or Bodhisattva must keep compassion as their main practice.

The second line likens the instructions on training the mind to the essence of nectar. The nectar enjoyed by gods and some humans produces only ordinary happiness, but the instructions on training the mind can provide the extraordinary bliss of full enlightenment.

The third line shows that from the many different instructions Atisha received and handed down through Dromtönpa and other Teachers to Geshe Chekhawa, this particular instruction came from his Spiritual Guide Serlingpa.

It is said that Geshe Chekhawa originally belonged to the old tradition of Tibetan Buddhism, the Nyingma tradition. Although he was well-versed in the teachings of both the old and the new traditions of Dharma, he was not entirely satisfied with his practice. He sought teachings from Rechungpa, one of Milarepa's main disciples, and later from the Kadampa Teacher Geshe Chagshinpa. One day, when in Geshe Chagshinpa's room, he found a short text entitled *Eight Verses of Training the Mind*. Two lines in the sixth verse caught his attention:

May I accept defeat
And offer the victory to others.

Even though he already possessed a profound knowledge of Dharma his mind was deeply affected by these words. Wanting to discover their real meaning he asked Geshe Chagshinpa the name of the author. Geshe Chagshinpa replied that the text was written by Geshe Langri Tangpa. Immediately upon hearing this, Geshe Chekhawa developed a wish to receive teachings from Geshe Langri Tangpa, and he set out at once for Lhasa where he hoped to meet him. When he arrived he discovered that Geshe Langri Tangpa had passed away and so he decided to find one of Geshe Langri Tangpa's disciples who could give him an explanation of this verse. He met a man from the province of Lang Tang who told him that one of Geshe Langri Tangpa's main disciples was Geshe Sharawa. Encouraged by this, Geshe Chekhawa set out to find Geshe Sharawa. When he found him, Geshe Sharawa was teaching a course on philosophy to a vast audience. Geshe Chekhawa listened to the teachings, which went on for several days, but he heard no mention of accepting defeat and offering the victory to others. After the teachings had finished, Geshe Chekhawa approached Geshe Sharawa as he was circumambulating a stupa and, putting his upper garment on the ground as a seat, requested him 'Please sit down for a while. I have something to ask you.' Geshe Sharawa replied rather abruptly 'I have just given extensive teachings from the throne, did you not understand them?' Geshe Chekhawa answered 'I have one special question.' Geshe Sharawa then sat down and Geshe Chekhawa asked 'How important is the practice of accepting defeat and offering the victory to others?' Geshe Sharawa replied 'If you want to attain enlightenment, this practice is essential.' Geshe Chekhawa then asked where this practice was taught in the scriptures, and Geshe Sharawa replied by quoting two lines from Nagarjuna's *Precious Garland of Advice for the King*:

> May their negative actions ripen upon me
> And may all my virtues ripen upon them.

Implicit in these words is the wish to accept defeat oneself and offer the victory to others. Geshe Sharawa gave further sources that convinced Geshe Chekhawa that this teaching was authentic. Geshe Chekhawa then requested Geshe Sharawa to give him full instructions on this practice. Geshe Sharawa replied 'If you stay with me for several years I will teach you.' Geshe Chekhawa stayed with Geshe Sharawa for twelve years, and within six years he had become very skilled at training his mind. Other Kadampa Geshes recognized that he had attained the Mahayana path of seeing by completely abandoning self-cherishing.

Until this time the instructions on training the mind had not been taught openly but had remained a secret lineage. Since it was necessary to possess a certain degree of faith before practising these instructions, Geshe Chekhawa at first taught them only to his closest and most receptive disciples.

This was a time when leprosy was widespread in Tibet because doctors were unable to cure it. One day Geshe Chekhawa met some lepers and decided to instruct them in the practice of training the mind, and especially in the practice of taking and giving. Through engaging in these practices many of the lepers were quickly cured of their disease. News of this spread rapidly and many other sufferers came to see Geshe Chekhawa, whose home soon took on the appearance of a hospital. As a result, Geshe Chekhawa's teachings became known among Tibetans as the 'Dharma for leprosy'.

Geshe Chekhawa had a brother who disliked Dharma intensely and had no faith in Geshe Chekhawa himself. One day he happened to overhear some of the teachings on training the mind that Geshe Chekhawa was giving to the lepers and was impressed by what he heard. Some time later Geshe Chekhawa noticed from his brother's behaviour that he was practising the instructions on training the mind. Geshe Chekhawa thought that if a disbeliever such as his brother could benefit from these teachings, many other beings could also be helped by them, and so he decided that it was no longer appropriate to keep the instructions secret. Accordingly, with a sincere wish to help all living beings, he composed the text *Training the Mind in Seven Points.* Because of his great kindness in composing this text and teaching it openly we now have an opportunity to receive these instructions and put them into practice. Therefore, we should remember with gratitude the kindness of Geshe Chekhawa.

It is like a diamond, like the sun, and like a medicinal tree.

The fourth line of Geshe Chekhawa's text explains the good qualities of the instructions on training the mind, likening them to a diamond, the sun, and a medicinal tree. Most precious things become valueless if they are broken, but if a diamond is cut into little pieces each fragment, however small, is still valuable. In this respect the instructions on training the mind are like a diamond because, while it is most valuable to practise all the instructions on training the mind, it is still very worthwhile to practise just some of them. Just as we would take care not to lose even the smallest fragment of a diamond, so we should not disregard any part of the instructions on training the mind, however small.

Just as full sunlight completely dispels all darkness but even a few rays provide a measure of light, so if we complete the practice of training the mind we shall totally dispel the darkness of our ignorance, but if we engage in only some parts of the practice this will still help to reduce our ignorance and self-cherishing.

Just as every part of a medicinal tree – the roots, trunk, branches, leaves, flowers, and fruit – provides medicine and is useful in curing disease, so every part of the instructions on training the mind can cure the mental disease of the delusions. Ordinary medicines can cure only physical disease, but the panacea of training the mind cures sicknesses of both body and mind. This is why the practice is sometimes called the 'unsurpassed medicine'.

How can we be sure that the instructions on training the mind really possess all these good qualities? This question is answered by Geshe Chekhawa in the fifth line of the root text:

The meaning of this text should be known.

Once we have understood the meaning of these instructions we should put them into practice. Then we shall come to understand all the excellent qualities of training the mind through our own experience. Unless we practise in this way we shall never know for ourself how these instructions are 'like a diamond, like the sun, and like a medicinal tree.'

The sixth and seventh lines of the root text reveal the power of training the mind to transform adverse conditions into the path to enlightenment:

The development of the five impurities
Will be transformed into the path to enlightenment.

It is said that this present age has five impurities: the impurity of time, the impurity of living beings, the impurity of view, the impurity of delusions, and the impurity of life span. The impurity of time is the relative poverty of spiritual practice at this time. There has been a great decline in spirituality through the ages, and human beings are now very poor in terms of their spiritual development compared with beings in the past. In ancient times many beings were spiritually so advanced that they could see Buddhas and Bodhisattvas directly. Many attained tranquil abiding and different kinds of clairvoyance, such as eye clairvoyance (the ability to see distant forms and subtle forms), ear clairvoyance (the ability to hear distant sounds far beyond the normal range), the mental power of knowing others' minds directly, and the mental power of knowing past and future lives. Many also possessed miracle powers, such as the ability to emanate different forms or the ability to fly. During this time countless beings attained liberation and enlightenment.

With the passing of time, however, fewer and fewer beings have been able to see Buddhas and Bodhisattvas directly, or to attain other high spiritual accomplishments. These days no ordinary being can see enlightened beings directly. The fact that we see everyone as ordinary is in itself a sign of the impurity of our times. However, if we practise training the mind purely we can turn these faults and imperfections of our times, which usually cause great difficulties and suffering, into causes of spiritual paths.

The impurity of living beings is the beings themselves. Living beings today experience very little peace and happiness, whereas external dangers to life are increasing greatly. Our natures are much grosser and our sufferings and difficulties far worse than those of beings in the past. With every passing generation living beings become more and more unhappy, more and more unruly, and more and more disturbed. We are now very skilled at producing all kinds of weapons for waging war and harming each other, but we lack the skills to create peace and happiness. Even though we long for peace and happiness we busily lay the foundations for conflict and suffering. We have made great advances in producing material things but these do not bring true peace, nor do they eradicate our sufferings permanently. However, if we practise training the mind purely we can transform all these adversities into causes of the path to enlightenment.

The impurity of view is the strong tendency of people these days to accept and foster mistaken or distorted views, such as views that deny past and future lives, the existence of enlightened beings, the functioning of karma, or the effectiveness of Dharma. If we practise training the mind purely we can eliminate all wrong views.

The impurity of delusions means that our anger, attachment, and ignorance are much stronger and more harmful than the delusions experienced by people of earlier times, and consequently our sufferings are far worse. Moreover, because we find it difficult to control our delusions our spiritual practice produces very few results. However, if we engage sincerely in the practice of training the mind we can transform the faults of these delusions into causes of spiritual paths.

The fifth impurity is impurity of life span. It is said that when Buddha Krakuchchanda appeared in this world human beings lived for long periods of time – about eighty thousand years. By the time of the second Buddha, Buddha Kanakamuni, life expectancy had diminished to forty thousand years, by the time of the third Buddha, Buddha Kashyapa, it had fallen to twenty thousand years, and by the time of the fourth Buddha, Buddha Shakyamuni, it was about one hundred years. In the scriptures it is said that this decline will continue until the average human life span is only ten years. However, if we use our human life to practise training the mind sincerely, we shall be able to attain the highest goal of full enlightenment within this short life.

The main reason for practising these instructions on training the mind is to fulfil our deepest wish – to attain lasting happiness and complete freedom from suffering. These cannot be attained by external means such as the acquisition of material wealth. No matter how many possessions we acquire, they will not provide us with any lasting happiness and freedom. On the contrary, it is often our pursuit of material possessions that causes our problems. If we want ultimate happiness and freedom from suffering we must engage in the supreme practices of training the mind. There is no other way.

All living beings have Buddha seed, or Buddha nature. The method that causes this seed to ripen is putting the instructions on training the mind into practice. The actual experiences, or realizations, of training the mind are the paths to enlightenment; therefore it is essential for all beings to gain experience of this practice. At the very end of the *Condensed Perfection of Wisdom Sutra* Buddha says:

> I have explained the paths to enlightenment so that all living beings might attain them.

Manjushri

Conventional Bodhichitta

THE PRELIMINARY PRACTICES OF TRAINING THE MIND

First learn the preliminaries

Before we can engage in the main practice of training the mind we must prepare our mind by engaging in the preliminary practices. The uncommon realizations of training the mind depend upon accumulating merit, purifying negativities, receiving the blessings of the Buddhas and Bodhisattvas, and training in the common practices of the stages of the path (Tib. Lamrim), from reliance upon our Spiritual Guide through to superior seeing. Within these it is particularly important to gain some experience of the meditations on this precious human life, impermanence and death, karma, and the dangers of samsara.

The supreme method for accumulating merit, purifying negativities, and receiving blessings from the Buddhas and Bodhisattvas is the six preparatory practices. These are:

(1) Cleaning the meditation room and setting up a shrine with representations of Buddha's body, speech, and mind.
(2) Arranging suitable offerings.
(3) Sitting in the correct meditation posture, going for refuge, and generating and enhancing bodhichitta.
(4) Visualizing the Field for Accumulating Merit.
(5) Accumulating merit and purifying negativity by offering the practice of the seven limbs and the mandala.
(6) Requesting the Field for Accumulating Merit in general and the Lamrim lineage Gurus in particular to bestow their blessings.

These are explained extensively in Lamrim texts such as *Joyful Path of Good Fortune*. The essence of these preparatory practices, and of all the common meditations on the stages of the path, is contained in *Essence of Good Fortune*, which can be found in Appendix IV. We should perform these preparatory practices with every meditation session on training the mind. We begin each session by reciting the prayers up to the end of the prayer of the stages of the path, and then we do our meditation on training the mind. After the meditation we recite the mantra and the dedication verses.

THE MAIN PRACTICE: TRAINING IN THE TWO BODHICHITTAS

The main practice of training the mind has two parts:

1 Training in conventional bodhichitta
2 Training in ultimate bodhichitta

There are two types of bodhichitta: conventional bodhichitta and ultimate bodhichitta. Usually the term 'bodhichitta', or 'mind of enlightenment', refers to conventional bodhichitta. Conventional bodhichitta is defined as a primary mind, motivated by great compassion, that spontaneously seeks enlightenment for the benefit of all living beings. It is a method for ripening our Buddha seed and is a collection of merit, the main cause of accomplishing the Form Body of a Buddha.

Ultimate bodhichitta is defined as a wisdom, motivated by conventional bodhichitta, that directly realizes emptiness, the ultimate nature of phenomena. It functions to remove the two obstructions – the obstructions to liberation and the obstructions to omniscience – and is a collection of wisdom, the main cause of accomplishing the Truth Body of a Buddha. If we practise these two bodhichittas we shall be travelling on the main path that leads to the state of full enlightenment.

TRAINING IN CONVENTIONAL BODHICHITTA

This has two parts:

1 The practice in the meditation session
2 The practice in the meditation break

THE PRACTICE IN THE MEDITATION SESSION

This has six parts:

1 Meditating on equalizing self and others
2 Contemplating the dangers of self-cherishing
3 Contemplating the benefits of cherishing others
4 Meditating on exchanging self with others
5 Meditating on taking and giving
6 Meditating on bodhichitta

MEDITATING ON EQUALIZING SELF AND OTHERS

Although this meditation is not explained explicitly in the root text of *Training the Mind in Seven Points*, it is implicitly included. A full explanation of this practice can be found in Shantideva's *Guide to the Bodhisattva's Way of Life*, where he says:

> First I should strive to meditate
> On equalizing self and others.
> Since we are equal from the point of view of suffering
> I should protect everyone as I do myself.

The meditation on equalizing self and others is one of the best methods for developing affectionate love, the very heart of the practice of training the mind. It is an extremely important practice because without the experience of equalizing self and others we cannot attain the realization of exchanging self with others.

What is it that we have to equalize in this meditation? We have to make our love for ourself and our love for others equal, cherishing ourself and others equally. This is impossible unless we are well-acquainted with Dharma. At present, when we think 'I' we feel that the object of this thought is supremely important; but when we think 'they' we consider that object to be far less important. This clearly shows that we do not cherish others as much as we cherish ourself. When we face difficulties or hard times we easily become depressed, yet rarely, if ever, do we feel upset about others' difficulties. Indeed, hearing of the misfortunes of certain individuals may even please us. This indicates that we have not yet equalized our love of self and our love of others.

We may wonder why equalizing ourself and others is so important. What will happen if we fail to do it? There will be two great faults. First we shall experience problems in this life. For example, if we fail to cherish others as much as ourself we may become angry with others and act in a selfish, negative way that will bring us unpleasant results. The second fault is that we shall not develop bodhichitta, and without bodhichitta we shall not be able to attain any realizations of the Mahayana path, let alone Buddhahood. Previous practitioners of Buddhism in India and Tibet realized that affectionate love is a special cause of bodhichitta.

It is important even for those who are not spiritual practitioners to practise equalizing self and others to some extent because, if they do not, they will certainly experience problems. For example, if we have a relationship with someone and we love and care for them we shall both be happy; but if we are concerned only with ourself our partner will soon become unhappy and our friendship will not last. If we do not learn to cherish others we shall not experience stable love, we shall find relationships difficult, and we shall not find real, lasting contentment. Therefore, we should always try to see others as precious and feel love and affection for them.

If we live in a community and have a caring attitude towards each other we shall naturally develop affectionate love, and as a result everyone will find peace and happiness. We should think 'Just as I want happiness for myself, so does everyone else. Therefore, I must work as hard for their happiness as I do for my own.' A person concerned for others in this way is equalizing self and others. If we maintain this intention with respect to others, they in turn will develop kind feelings towards us. First we should try to practise this with our friends and those with whom we associate regularly, and then, when we have some experience of this, extend our practice until eventually we can encompass all other beings.

When we first attempt this meditation we may develop doubts and question the value of trying to remove the sufferings of others. We may think: 'No one else's suffering directly affects me. Each of us has to bear our own suffering, so why should I try to dispel the suffering of others?' While it is true that we do not experience others' suffering directly, this does not mean that we should not try to help them. If we have a thorn in our foot, our hand will pull it out even though it is not directly affected. In the same way, if we think of all living beings as one body, united in wishing to be free from suffering, we shall not hesitate in trying to alleviate their sufferings. We should think:

Just as I want lasting happiness, so do all other beings. In this way we are all exactly the same. Is it not unreasonable to seek my own happiness but neglect the happiness of others?

Equalizing self and others is the foundation of all the subsequent practices that lead to enlightenment. Therefore, we should encourage ourself by contemplating:

Now I have attained a rare and precious human life. Not to use it to attain Buddhahood would be a tragic waste of a golden opportunity. To attain enlightenment I need to equalize myself and others. Then I shall be able to train in the practices of taking and giving, develop the precious minds of compassion and bodhichitta, and eventually attain enlightenment.

To do the actual meditation on equalizing ourself and others we should begin by considering all the preceding points carefully until we become convinced that others' welfare is as important as our own. This will lead to a feeling of equality between ourself and others. We concentrate on this feeling for a while and then we make the resolution 'I will cherish others as much as I cherish myself.' We meditate on this resolution for as long as possible.

When we rise from meditation, throughout the rest of the day we should repeatedly recall the feelings and determinations we developed during meditation. Whenever we see someone in pain or experiencing difficulties we should try to respond by helping them. If we cannot help in a practical way we should at least try to help with our thoughts and prayers. For example, although we alone cannot bring about peace when two nations are at war we can nevertheless feel concern for all those involved and pray that peace will soon be restored. We can also dedicate our virtuous actions for their benefit, thinking 'Through the virtues of this action may their conflict cease.' In general, we can direct the merit of our virtuous actions to any good cause, and this will indirectly help to solve many problems.

If we continuously maintain a wish to help others we shall always find ways to help them, either directly or indirectly. As Nagarjuna says in *Commentary on Bodhichitta*:

> Even if we are not able to help others directly
> We should still try to develop a beneficial intention.
> If we develop this intention more and more strongly,
> We shall naturally find ways to help others.

We can help others only if we have the wish to do so, therefore we should cultivate a beneficial intention again and again. If we keep this beneficial thought in mind throughout all our daily activities we shall find that opportunities to help others will occur more and more frequently.

It is also essential to make repeated requests to all the Buddhas, Bodhisattvas, and other holy beings to grant us their blessings so that we may attain the realization of cherishing ourself and others equally. We can do this by reciting the following prayer from *Offering to the Spiritual Guide*:

> *In that no one wishes for even the slightest suffering,*
> *Or is ever content with the happiness they have,*

There is no difference between myself and others;
Realizing this, I seek your blessings joyfully to make
others happy.

This chapter presents a sequence of meditations, beginning with this meditation on equalizing self and others. We should spend as much time as we wish on each meditation. If we like, we can spend weeks, months, or even years on just this meditation.

CONTEMPLATING THE DANGERS OF SELF-CHERISHING

Gather all blame into one

This line shows that all sufferings and difficulties can be traced back to one source, the self-cherishing mind, and that it is this mind alone that we should blame for all our troubles. Because we cherish ourself we naturally want all the good things in life, and to obtain them we engage in selfish actions. In this way our self-cherishing leads us to commit actions that throw us again and again into samsaric rebirths; and each time we take rebirth in samsara we have to experience all its miseries again. If we did not have this self-cherishing mind we would not commit such unskilful actions, and then we would not have to experience their unpleasant effects.

Living beings commit negative actions such as killing out of concern for their own welfare. Most animals, for example, intent on their own survival, pursue and kill other animals for food. Similarly, human beings often become angry when others harm them or threaten them. If we decide to retaliate it is only because we consider ourself to be so precious. When a thief is caught and sent to prison we say that he has been imprisoned for committing a crime, but the main cause of his imprisonment is his self-cherishing mind. If we become unhappy because we want something but cannot obtain it, this is because in the past our self-cherishing mind prevented others from getting what they wanted. In previous lives, out of selfishness, we have caused physical and mental pain to others and we have prevented others from fulfilling their

Shantideva

wishes. Because of this we now experience difficulty in fulfilling our own wishes, we are burdened with an unhealthy body and mind, and we encounter many other obstacles. All these problems are caused by our self-cherishing.

If we consider this carefully we shall see that there is not a single fault that is not caused by self-cherishing. Therefore, we should decide very firmly to eliminate it. Buddha said:

> Look at samsara; it has no good qualities.
> Due to the enemy, self-cherishing,
> A hungry tigress
> Will even devour her own young.

In *Guide to the Bodhisattva's Way of Life* Shantideva says:

> If all the harm, all the fear,
> And all the suffering in this world
> Arise from self-grasping,
> What need have I for such a great demon?

Sometimes Shantideva refers to the self-grasping mind and sometimes he refers to the self-cherishing mind. What is the difference? The self-grasping mind apprehends or grasps the I as inherently existent, and the self-cherishing mind cherishes that I, holding it very dear. These two minds are the root of all our troubles.

Since we have always cherished ourself greatly we find it difficult to bear even the slightest problem, and so we constantly suffer from anxiety, fear, and unhappiness. All the mental pain that arises from unfulfilled wishes and from meeting unattractive objects is caused by self-cherishing. Superior Bodhisattvas have no self-cherishing and so they are not afraid of anything. They could face the fiercest tiger without fear. Since they look upon all beings as their mothers they feel compassion, not fear, when confronted with wild animals. This does not mean that they do not protect themselves from unnecessary injury. One of the qualities of high Bodhisattvas is that they are able happily to give their body or parts of their body to others, but before doing so they consider the situation carefully and make the sacrifice only if they think the action will be beneficial. Similarly, we should take care not to expose ourself to unnecessary risk or danger. If there is no benefit to anyone there is no point in our risking injury or death. We should not think that protecting ourself is necessarily a sign of self-cherishing.

When we contemplate the dangers of self-cherishing we may develop doubts, thinking that without self-cherishing we would have no motive to work, without work we would have no money, and without money we would not be able to survive; and we might conclude that it is only through the kindness of the self-cherishing mind that we survive at all. In fact, the wish to work does not necessarily depend upon having a self-cherishing attitude. There are many altruistic people in the world who work primarily for others. Sincere Dharma practitioners wish to work to provide themselves with the basic necessities of life so that they have the energy to practise Dharma. Their ultimate aim is to attain enlightenment for the sake of all living beings.

At times we may think that the people who appear most successful in life owe their success to the power of self-cherishing. Motivated by ambition and self-cherishing they have worked hard, and now they are enjoying the rewards. If we think like this we have not properly understood the relationship between actions and their effects. We have to be clear about precisely which effect follows upon which action. A bankrupt businessman can be as strongly self-cherishing as a successful one. If self-cherishing were the key to success, how could one be bankrupt and the other wealthy? Buddha taught that the cause of wealth is giving. Thus, the difference between a successful businessman and a failed businessman is that the former practised giving in previous lives whereas the latter did not. Whenever doubts on this subject arise we should check them carefully. If we apply sound logical reasoning we shall be able to resolve all our misgivings.

To do this meditation we should try to become fully aware of the dangers of self-cherishing and conclude by resolving to abandon it completely. We should then meditate on this resolution single-pointedly, without distraction.

During the meditation break we should remain mindful of this resolution. Although we cannot eliminate our self-cherishing mind just by resolving to do so, maintaining this continuous aspiration will help us greatly. We should also make repeated requests to all the Buddhas, Bodhisattvas, and other holy beings to grant us their blessings so that we may be able to overcome our self-cherishing. We can do this by reciting the following prayer from *Offering to the Spiritual Guide*:

Seeing that this chronic disease of cherishing myself
Is the cause that gives rise to unwanted suffering,
I seek your blessings to destroy this great demon of selfishness
By resenting it as the object of blame.

CONTEMPLATING THE BENEFITS OF CHERISHING OTHERS

Meditate on the great kindness of all

The precious human body that we now possess was gained through the kindness of other living beings. Likewise, the pleasures we enjoy as humans are provided by the kindness of others; our education, understanding, skills, experience, and so forth were achieved through the kindness of others; the opportunity to listen to, contemplate, and meditate on Dharma is provided through the kindness of others; and liberation and enlightenment are attained through the kindness of others. If we meditate in this way we shall become deeply convinced of the kindness of all other beings towards us.

Since the principal causes of gaining a human rebirth are the practices of moral discipline, giving, and patience, we must have practised these in the past. Who were the objects of these practices? Other living beings. Without them we would not have been able to create the causes of a human rebirth. It is through their kindness that we have attained this precious human life, which is more meaningful than a whole universe full of jewels.

Our day-to-day needs are provided through the kindness of others. We brought nothing with us from our former lives, yet as soon as we were born we were given a home, food, clothes, and everything we needed; all provided by the kindness of others. Everything we now enjoy has been provided through the generosity of other beings, past or present. We are able to make use of many things with very little effort on our own part. If we consider facilities such as roads, houses, cars, trains, aeroplanes, ships, restaurants, hotels, libraries, museums, and shops, it will become clear that many people worked very hard and underwent great difficulties to provide these things. We may think that it is not due to the kindness of others that we can use these things but because we pay to do so; but where does our money come from? It does not fall from the sky or grow on trees; it is provided by others. We may still feel that money is not just given to us but earned by our hard work, but our work is provided by others. Someone has to employ us or do business with us. Being provided with work or business is like being provided with money.

If we check carefully it becomes clearer how others help us through their kindness. By checking in this way we should come to the conclusion 'I must cherish other living beings because they are so kind.' With this determination we should try to generate a mind that holds all beings equally dear, and then sustain this loving mind in single-pointed meditation.

If we think clearly we shall also understand that all our present and future happiness depend upon our cherishing others. How is this? In past lives we avoided harming, killing, or stealing from those whom we cared for; and we were generous and patient with them because we loved them. As a result of these positive actions we have now attained this precious human life. Sometimes in the past we also helped and protected others because we cared for them, and as a result we now receive help and enjoy pleasant conditions.

If we practise cherishing others sincerely in this life we shall resolve our many problems of anger, jealousy, and so forth, and our mind will always be calm and peaceful. Cherishing others brings them happiness and prevents conflicts and disputes. If we cherish others we shall avoid harming them with negative actions. Instead we shall practise positive actions of love, patience, and giving, and thereby create the cause to experience happiness and good fortune in the future. Furthermore, if we make cherishing others our main practice we shall gradually develop great compassion and bodhichitta. Eventually we shall attain the ultimate happiness of great enlightenment.

By contemplating in this way we shall arrive at the following decision: 'I must always cherish other beings because this precious mind of love will bring happiness to myself and others.' Then we hold this thought and meditate on it single-pointedly for as long as possible. During the meditation break we should try to keep this attitude in mind all the time, whatever we are doing.

It is very important to request all the holy beings to grant us their blessings so that we may gain experience of the precious mind that cherishes all living beings. We can do this by reciting the following prayer from *Offering to the Spiritual Guide*:

Seeing that the mind that cherishes mother beings and
would secure their happiness
Is the gateway that leads to infinite good qualities,
I seek your blessings to cherish these beings more than
my life,
Even if they rise up against me as my enemies.

MEDITATING ON EXCHANGING SELF WITH OTHERS

The main reason for explaining the many dangers of self-cherishing and the many benefits of cherishing others is that through contemplating them carefully again and again we shall be able to exchange self with others. Exchanging self with others does not mean that we become someone else and they become us. What we exchange is the object of our cherishing. At present we ourself are the object of our cherishing mind, but when we exchange self with others the object of our cherishing becomes other sentient beings.

We need to exchange self with others because self-cherishing is the root of all our problems, whereas the mind that

Serlingpa

cherishes others is the source of all goodness. Through this practice we shall find both temporary and ultimate happiness. In *Guide to the Bodhisattva's Way of Life* Shantideva says:

> The childish work for their own benefit,
> The Buddhas work for the benefit of others.
> Just look at the difference between them!

Here 'the childish' refers to ordinary beings who, motivated by self-interest, achieve nothing but suffering; whereas the Buddhas, who constantly work for others, have attained enlightenment and are totally free from suffering. Seeing the difference between them we should resolve to cherish others more than ourself because we need to attain enlightenment.

We should not be discouraged by thinking that exchanging self with others is too difficult for us. In *Guide to the Bodhisattva's Way of Life* Shantideva says that even extremely difficult things such as cherishing our most bitter enemy become easy through the power of familiarity, therefore if we practise sincerely and patiently we shall definitely be able to exchange self with others eventually.

The body that we now cherish does not actually belong to us but arose from a mixture of our father's sperm and our mother's ovum. However, we think of it as our own body because we are so familiar with it. Just as we have become used to cherishing this body as our own when in fact it belongs to our parents, so we can take others as our object of cherishing and gradually become used to this idea until, through the power of complete familiarity, it becomes easy for us to cherish others instead of ourself.

Take my own case as an example. When I was an eight year old novice monk I cherished the body of a novice monk, and when I became a fully ordained monk at the age of twenty-one I cherished the body of a young fully ordained monk. When I am eighty years old I shall cherish the body of an old fully ordained monk. We think that the observed body remains the same, but it does not. When I became a monk the body of the lay boy ceased. The object of cherishing changes year by year, and because the object changes the thought 'I' changes. Last year's person, for example, has now ceased completely. Since the object of our cherishing changes naturally in this way, there is no reason why we cannot change our object of cherishing to other living beings. Developing a mind that cherishes others depends upon effort, familiarity, and practice.

By contemplating these points we should develop a strong determination to cherish only other living beings, and then concentrate on this determination single-pointedly for as long as possible.

It is better to begin by cherishing our friends and relatives and then gradually to extend this to include all living beings. We cannot accomplish this quickly, but with perseverance we shall succeed. We need to maintain this feeling of cherishing others throughout our meditation break and practise it together with all our daily activities. The measurement of having gained the realization of exchanging self with others is that in every situation we naturally cherish others more than ourself.

It is essential to request all the Buddhas, Bodhisattvas, and other holy beings to grant us their blessings so that we may gain the realization of exchanging self with others. We can do this by reciting the following prayer from *Offering to the Spiritual Guide*:

Since cherishing myself is the door to all faults
And cherishing mother beings is the foundation of all good qualities,
I seek your blessings to take as my essential practice
The yoga of exchanging self with others.

MEDITATING ON TAKING AND GIVING

Train alternately in giving and taking

This meditation has two parts:

1 Taking by means of compassion
2 Giving by means of love

We practise taking and giving alternately. Here, 'taking' means taking the suffering of others upon ourself and 'giving' means giving them all our happiness. Since it is impossible for living beings to enjoy pure happiness while they are experiencing suffering we begin with the practice of taking, and then we practise giving.

TAKING BY MEANS OF COMPASSION

We practise taking with the motivation of compassion. We all feel compassion at some time or other; this is our Buddha nature. For example, there is no one who does not feel sympathy for their children, parents, or friends when they are experiencing suffering; and there are some with very virtuous tendencies who feel compassion even for strangers. If we gradually extend the scope of our compassion, eventually we shall develop spontaneous compassion for all living beings. A mind that wishes to protect all living beings from suffering is great compassion. If we develop this mind and gradually improve it, eventually it will become the compassion of a Buddha. Only a Buddha's compassion possesses the power actually to protect all living beings from suffering. The way to attain enlightenment, therefore, is to cultivate our present mind of compassion and develop it to the full.

Compassion is the root of a Buddha because all Buddhas arise from the mind of compassion; it is the root of Dharma because Buddhas give Dharma teachings out of compassion for others; and it is the root of Sangha because it is impossible to become Sangha without practising compassion. The great Mongolian meditator and highly respected scholar, Lama Tayang, wrote a poem praising compassion called *Precious Crystal Rosary*. In it he says:

> Compassion is the mother of all Buddhas,
> Compassion is the most precious treasure of
> Bodhisattvas,
> Compassion is the unseen friend of migrators;
> May I be protected by great compassion.

Buddhas are not enlightened from the beginning; they were once ordinary beings who, like us, had the seeds of compassion. By practising the correct methods they increased their compassion, making it more and more powerful, until finally it transformed into the ultimate compassion of a Buddha. This is why Lama Tayang says that compassion is the 'mother of all Buddhas'. If we want to become enlightened we should do as the previous Buddhas have done and increase our present mind of compassion. However, it is impossible to increase our compassion without knowing the correct methods and putting them into practice.

Bodhisattvas enter the spiritual path of the Mahayana out of great compassion, and throughout their training all their actions are motivated by compassion. Finally, through the power of their compassion they attain enlightenment. This is why they regard compassion as their 'most precious treasure'.

Compassion actually helps and protects living beings, but since they cannot see this directly it is called the 'unseen friend of migrators'. If we have great compassion we shall have nothing more to fear from samsara, and there will be no danger of our falling into the lower realms. We shall advance from joy to joy until finally we attain full enlightenment. Thus, compassion is the actual refuge and protector of all living beings.

If a mother sees her little child in pain she feels compassion because she loves her child; but if she were to see her enemies in trouble she might feel no compassion at all because she does not love them. If she had an unbiased mind cherishing all living beings she would instinctively feel the same compassion for her enemy as she does for her child. We should strive to develop such unbiased compassion for all living beings. To do this we must first extend our mind of cherishing others until we feel cherishing love for all living beings. Then if we contemplate their suffering we shall naturally develop compassion for them.

Instead of being concerned with our own problems, which serves only to make us depressed and unhappy, we should consider the difficulties of others. In this way we shall begin to feel sympathy for them. If we apply this to everyone we meet – friends, neighbours, strangers, rich or poor – we shall find that every ordinary being has problems. Even those who suffer the least still have to experience the sufferings of birth, sickness, ageing, death, frustrated desires, and unpleasant conditions; and everyone has to endure extreme sufferings at one time or another. On television and in the newspapers we see people experiencing terrible sufferings all the time. Even heads of state and the very wealthy are not exempt. Although we may envy such people and think that they must be happy with their status and wealth, in reality they are not. They experience many more problems and worries than those with less status and wealth because of their greater responsibilities; and they may even face physical danger because of it.

The way to meditate on great compassion is first to develop a mind of love that cherishes all living beings and then, with this mind, to contemplate their suffering again and again. Eventually a feeling of compassion will arise and we shall think 'How wonderful it would be if I could free all these living beings from their suffering.' When this feeling arises we maintain it by meditating on it single-pointedly for as long as possible.

It is also very important to make repeated requests to all the Buddhas, Bodhisattvas, and other holy beings to grant us their blessings so that we may generate great compassion. We can do this by reciting the following prayer from *Offering to the Spiritual Guide*:

Contemplating how all these pitiful migrators are my mothers,
Who out of kindness have cherished me again and again,
I seek your blessings to generate a spontaneous compassion
Like that of a loving mother for her dearest child.

Atisha

Begin the sequence by taking from your own side

To meditate on taking we begin by developing a feeling of compassion for all living beings as just explained, and let our whole mind become one with this compassion. Then we begin the actual meditation on taking the sufferings of others. At first we may find it difficult to take on others' sufferings, particularly the suffering of our enemies, but this will become easier as our compassion increases. The line from the root text quoted above advises us that if at first we find it difficult to take on others' suffering, we can begin by taking on our own future sufferings. We do not need to take on our past sufferings, only those that we shall have to experience between now and attaining liberation from samsara. First we make the resolution:

> *With this present mind and body I will take on all my future sufferings. By doing this I shall purify all my negative karma and thereby avoid having to experience these sufferings in the future. Then I shall be able gradually to take on the sufferings of others.*

Having made this resolution we imagine that all the sufferings we shall have to experience in the remainder of this life, such as the sufferings of sickness, old age, and death, assume the aspect of black smoke. This gathers into one great mass and dissolves into our heart, and we strongly imagine that it destroys our self-cherishing mind and our negative karma. Then we visualize all the sufferings of our future lives dissolving into our heart as black smoke, once again completely destroying our self-cherishing mind and our negative karma. We develop the conviction that we have destroyed our self-cherishing mind and purified our negative karma, and then generate joy. We meditate on this feeling of joy for as long as possible.

When we feel ready to begin taking on the sufferings of others, there are two ways in which we can do this. Either we can focus on all living beings in general and imagine taking on their sufferings, or we can focus on an individual being or on a specific group of beings and imagine taking on their particular sufferings.

To practise the first method we regard all living beings as our kind mothers and think:

All these mother beings are drowning in samsara's ocean, experiencing unbearable miseries repeatedly over a long period of time. How wonderful it would be if they could be released from this deep ocean of suffering. May they be released. I myself will release them.

With this strong compassionate motivation we think:

May the sufferings and negative karma of all living beings ripen upon me and thus may they all experience instant release from suffering and its causes.

With this strong prayer we imagine that the suffering and negative karma of all living beings gather together in the aspect of black smoke, which dissolves into our heart and completely destroys our self-cherishing. We develop the strong conviction 'I have now released all living beings from the ocean of samsara and have destroyed my self-cherishing mind.' We hold this conviction for a while and then generate joy. We meditate single-pointedly on this joy for as long as possible.

The second method is to focus on specific groups of beings, such as the beings who inhabit each of the six realms of samsara, and imagine taking on their particular sufferings. We begin by focusing on the beings suffering in the hot hells and think:

These beings, who are all my kind mothers, have no choice but to experience the torment of extreme heat for many aeons. How wonderful it would be if they could be released from these terrible sufferings as quickly as possible. May they be released. I myself will release them.

With this compassionate mind we think:

May I take on all their suffering and negative karma, and as a result may they be completely released from suffering and its causes.

With this heartfelt prayer we imagine that all their suffering and negative karma gather together in the aspect of black smoke, which dissolves into our heart and completely destroys our self-cherishing. We develop the conviction 'I have now released all beings in the hot hells from their suffering and have destroyed my self-cherishing mind.' We hold this conviction for a while and then generate joy. We meditate on this joy for as long as possible.

To take on the sufferings of the beings in the cold hells we focus on them and think:

> *All these mother beings have to experience the unbearable suffering of cold for many aeons. How wonderful it would be if they could be released from this suffering. May they be released. I myself will release them.*

With this sincere prayer we imagine that all their suffering and negative karma gather together in the aspect of black smoke, which dissolves into our heart and completely destroys our self-cherishing. We develop the conviction 'I have now released all beings in the cold hells from their suffering and have destroyed my self-cherishing mind.' We hold this conviction for a while and then generate joy. We meditate on this joy for as long as possible.

Then we focus on the beings of the hungry ghost realm. Remembering how they are all our mothers, we contemplate how they now have to experience the pain and misery of intense hunger for many aeons. Feeling great pity for them we think:

> *How wonderful it would be if they no longer had to endure such sufferings. May they be released from suffering. I myself will release them.*

With this compassionate mind we make the strong prayer:

> *May all their sufferings of hunger and thirst and their non-virtuous karma ripen upon me so that they may be released from suffering and its causes.*

We imagine that all their suffering and negative karma gather together in the aspect of black smoke, which dissolves into our heart and completely destroys our self-cherishing. We develop the conviction 'I have now released all the hungry ghosts from their suffering and have destroyed my self-cherishing mind.' We hold this conviction for a while and then generate joy. We hold this feeling with mindfulness for as long as possible.

Then we focus on the beings of the animal realm and think:

> *All these pitiful mother beings are compelled to experience deep ignorance, ill-treatment, exploitation by humans, imprisonment, slaughter, and many other fears and miseries. How wonderful it would be if they could be released from this suffering. May they be released. I myself will release them.*

We imagine that all their suffering and negative karma gather together in the aspect of black smoke, which dissolves into our heart and completely destroys our self-cherishing. At the same time all animals are released from every suffering and its cause. We develop the conviction that as a result of our practice of taking they have been completely freed and now experience only peace and happiness; and that we ourself have become free from self-cherishing. We hold this conviction for a while and then generate joy. We meditate on this joy for as long as possible.

Then we focus on the beings of the human realm and think:

> *All human beings, whether they are my friends, my enemies, or strangers, have to experience without any choice countless sufferings such as birth, ageing, illness, pain, and death. How wonderful it would be if they could be released from these miseries. May they be released. I myself will release them. May all their sufferings and negative karma ripen upon me now.*

We imagine that all their suffering and negative karma gather together in the aspect of black smoke, which dissolves into our heart and completely destroys our self-cherishing. We develop the conviction 'I have now released all human beings from their specific and general sufferings, and have destroyed my self-cherishing mind.' We hold this conviction for a while and then generate joy. We meditate on this joy for as long as possible.

Then we focus on the beings of the demi-god realm and think:

> *Each of these beings is my kind mother, but now they have to experience the sufferings of jealousy and conflict. How wonderful it would be if they could be released from this suffering. May they be released. I myself will release them. Due to my taking on their suffering and negative karma, may they become free from their misery.*

We imagine that all their jealousy, aggression, pain, and misery gather together in the aspect of black smoke, which dissolves into our heart and completely destroys our self-cherishing. We develop the conviction 'I have now released all these beings from their suffering and have destroyed my self-cherishing mind.' We hold this conviction for a while and then generate joy. We meditate on this joy for as long as possible.

Then we focus on the beings of the god realms and think:

> *All these beings are my dear mothers, but, because of their contaminated aggregates, as death approaches they have to experience the suffering of losing their vitality, magnificence, and happiness. How wonderful it would be if they could be released from their fears and suffering. May they be released. I myself will release them. May their suffering and its causes ripen upon me now.*

We imagine that all their suffering and contaminated karma gather together in the aspect of black smoke, which dissolves into our heart and completely destroys our self-cherishing. We develop the conviction 'I have now released all the gods from their suffering and its causes and have destroyed my self-cherishing mind.' We hold this conviction for a while and then generate joy. We meditate on this joy for as long as possible.

This is the way to practise taking the suffering of all beings of the six realms. Within each realm there are individual and specific sufferings to contemplate. For example, when we focus on human beings' suffering we can focus on the sufferings of a particular sick person, on a group of people who suffer from a particular disease, or on all sick people in general. We can also focus on those who suffer from famine, drought, poverty, war, accidents, disasters, and so on. Having chosen our object we develop a mind of strong compassion, make prayers, and resolve to remove these sufferings. Then we practise taking in the way that has been explained. The same method can be applied to any situation we can imagine.

If we are unfamiliar with this practice we should begin by focusing on our parents, children, friends, and relatives. We can then gradually broaden our focus to include our neighbours, those living in the locality, everyone in the country, all human beings, and finally all beings of the six realms.

At the conclusion of each meditation session we make the following dedication:

> *Through the power of these virtues may each and every living being be released from suffering, negative karma, danger, and fear.*

We can make general dedications or dedications for specific purposes, as we wish.

Generally we can purify negative karma in two ways: by engaging in specific purification practices or by experiencing suffering. Milarepa provides an example of the second way. Early in his life he created very heavy negative karma by killing many people. Later his Spiritual Guide, Marpa, allowed him to undergo many difficulties that entailed severe suffering. This suffering was the actual means by which he purified all his negativities. In Tibet there is a saying that suffering is like a broom that sweeps away negativities. The practice of taking on the sufferings of others is a supreme method for purifying non-virtuous karma, accumulating merit, and improving our compassion.

GIVING BY MEANS OF LOVE

There are three kinds of love: affectionate love, cherishing love, and wishing love. We can understand these by considering the following example. If a mother is reunited with one of her children after a long separation she is very happy and feels great affection for her. This special feeling of affection is affectionate love. Out of affection the mother considers her child to be very precious and wants to take special care of her. This special feeling of caring is cherishing love. Because she has affectionate love and cherishing love for her child, if she sees that she is unhappy she will immediately wish to restore her happiness. This wish for others to be happy and to help them to achieve happiness is wishing love.

First we need to generate affectionate love and then cherishing love for other living beings. Then if we meditate on their lack of happiness we shall naturally develop wishing love. It is this wishing love that is our motivation for engaging in the practice of giving. Motivated by such love we resolve 'I will give happiness to all living beings.'

In *Guide to the Bodhisattva's Way of Life* Shantideva explains how to meditate on giving:

> To benefit all living beings
> Transform your body into a wishfulfilling jewel.

We begin by thinking:

> *May my virtuous karma ripen upon all living beings, and thus may they attain both temporary and ultimate happiness.*

With this strong prayer we imagine that our body transforms into a wishfulfilling jewel, sparkling with light, whose rays reach all six realms of samsara. These rays purify all environments throughout the six realms and bestow upon all the beings inhabiting them everything they could possibly desire. The beings in the hot hells receive cooling rain, those in the

Dromtönpa

cold hells receive warming sunshine, hungry ghosts receive food and drink, animals receive wisdom, humans fulfil all their wishes and needs, demi-gods receive peace and satisfaction, and gods gain freedom. We develop the conviction that they are all fully satisfied and experiencing uncontaminated bliss; and we generate a feeling of great joy at their newly found happiness. We then maintain this feeling of joy by meditating single-pointedly on it for as long as possible. This meditation on giving happiness to others is a supreme method for accumulating merit and increasing our mind of love.

Mount these two upon the breath

Once we have mastered the practices of taking and giving we shall be able to combine them with our breathing. This will make our practice much more powerful. How is this done? As we inhale we generate strong compassion for all living beings and think that we are drawing in all their sufferings in the aspect of black smoke. This smoke enters our nostrils and descends to our heart, where it completely destroys our self-cherishing mind. We hold our breath for a moment and think 'Now all living beings are freed from suffering, and my negative karma and self-cherishing mind are completely purified.' As we breathe out, with a strong motivation of love we think 'I am giving my happiness and good qualities to all living beings', and we imagine that we exhale rays of light which are in essence all our present and future happiness. We develop the conviction that as a result of our practice all living beings experience pure happiness.

There is a very close relationship between our mind and our inner energy winds. When the practice of taking and giving is mounted upon the breath it is connected with our inner winds and so it helps to control them and thereby control the mind. When we become thoroughly familiar with this practice our ordinary breathing, even during sleep, will be transformed into the practice of taking and giving, and the very process of breathing will become meaningful. Geshe

Chekhawa, Je Tsongkhapa, and many other great Yogis were able to transform breathing in this way. When we have become completely familiar with taking and giving we shall be able to mount the practice upon the breath wherever we are and whatever we are doing – standing, sitting, walking, or lying down – and this will help us to develop extremely stable and refined states of concentration.

The practice of taking and giving can also be very helpful in curing sickness. Even someone with an incurable disease who practises taking and giving, emphasizing in particular the practice of taking, can experience a remission or even a complete cure. For example, if we have cancer we should bring to mind all the beings in the world who are also suffering from cancer at this moment. We think about them for a while and try to develop strong compassion. Then we make the decision:

> *I will take the sickness of cancer from every one of these beings so that they may be released from the suffering of this disease.*

We then visualize all their cancer in the aspect of black smoke leaving each individual and absorbing into our own cancer. We think that because we have done this all those beings are now perfectly healthy again. Can this technique actually cure cancer? Yes, because taking on the sickness and suffering of those with cancer with a mind of compassion will purify the negative actions that cause the continuation of our own cancer. It is very difficult for the medical profession to cure cancer, but if someone with cancer purifies the negative actions that cause its development he or she can be cured. The practice of taking and giving is extremely helpful in all cases of degenerative illness. This is one of the reasons why Geshe Chekhawa was able to help lepers cure themselves. There have been many cases in Tibet of sick people who, having been diagnosed as incurable by their doctors, gave away all their belongings, left home, and went to the cemetery to die; but in the cemetery they practised taking and giving with deep concentration and, instead of dying, returned home fully recovered!

Before doing meditation on taking and giving we should offer a mandala with faith to all the Buddhas, Bodhisattvas, and other holy beings, and then request their blessings so that we may gain a special experience of this practice. We can do this by reciting three times the following precious verse from *Offering to the Spiritual Guide*:

Therefore, O Compassionate, Venerable Guru, I seek your blessings
So that all the suffering, negativities, and obstructions of mother sentient beings
Will ripen upon me right now;
And through my giving my happiness and virtue to others,
May all migrating beings be happy.

MEDITATING ON BODHICHITTA

We engage in the practices of taking and giving with a mind of great compassion and great love, wishing to free all living beings from suffering and to bestow upon them true happiness. However, wishing alone is not enough. If our child were to fall into the sea and start to drown it would not be enough simply to wish, however fervently, that she be saved – we would have to do something practical to rescue her. In a similar way, once we have developed a mind of great compassion that wishes to protect all living beings from suffering we shall recognize that this wish alone is insufficient to protect them. We must decide to act to free all living beings from their suffering. Keeping this resolve in mind, we meditate on it for as long as possible. This is known as 'training in superior intention'.

We then ask ourself 'Even though I want to, do I have the power to protect all living beings?' After careful consideration we shall realize that it is only enlightened beings who have this power because only they are completely free from all obstructions and have impartial compassion, and only they have the skilful means to help all living beings in many different ways, bestowing their help without partiality. Realizing this, we make the decision 'I must attain enlightenment for the sake of all living beings.' This mind is bodhichitta. We should hold it firmly and meditate on it for as long as possible.

When we first generate bodhichitta it is called 'artificial bodhichitta' because it is generated through effort, but if we continue to improve our bodhichitta through meditation, eventually it will arise naturally without effort. This spontaneous bodhichitta is actual bodhichitta.

While we are training in bodhichitta it is important that we prevent this special wish from degenerating. We can do this by engaging in the following practice each day. We visualize all the Buddhas, Bodhisattvas, and other holy beings in front of us and make the following promise three times:

From this time forth until I become a Buddha,
I shall keep even at the cost of my life
A mind wishing to attain complete enlightenment
To free all living beings from the fears of samsara and
solitary peace.

This practice makes our bodhichitta firm and prevents it from degenerating.

The next step is to take the Bodhisattva vows. To do this we visualize the assembly of Buddhas, Bodhisattvas, and other holy beings in front of us and, with compassion for all living beings, we think: 'I must attain enlightenment for the sake of all living beings. To accomplish this I will take the Bodhisattva vows and practise the six perfections.' With this motivation we then take the Bodhisattva vows by reciting the following prayer three times:

O Gurus, Buddhas, and Bodhisattvas
Please listen to what I now say.
Just as all the previous Sugatas
Generated the mind of enlightenment
And accomplished all the stages
Of the Bodhisattva training,
So will I too for the sake of all beings
Generate the mind of enlightenment

And accomplish all the stages
Of the Bodhisattva training.

After taking the Bodhisattva vows in this way we should train in the six perfections with bodhichitta motivation. All the Bodhisattva's practices are included within the six perfections: the perfections of giving, moral discipline, patience, effort, mental stabilization, and wisdom. By gradually improving our practice of the six perfections we shall eventually attain great enlightenment. The six perfections are very extensive and extremely profound but we can train in them gradually by sincerely practising the eighteen commitments and twenty-two precepts of training the mind with bodhichitta motivation. These commitments and precepts will be explained below.

THE PRACTICE IN THE MEDITATION BREAK

The three objects, three poisons, and three virtuous roots
Are the brief instruction for the subsequent attainment.

Here the 'three objects' are attractive, unattractive, and neutral objects. Every object that we perceive is included within these three. The 'three poisons' are desirous attachment, hatred, and ignorance, and the 'three virtuous roots' are non-attachment, non-hatred, and non-ignorance. 'Subsequent attainment' means our practice during the meditation break.

Non-attachment is a special virtuous mind that opposes desirous attachment, it is not simply the lack of attachment. Non-attachment is a virtuous mind whereas the mere lack of attachment is not necessarily a virtuous mind. For example, a baby lacks desirous attachment for alcohol but this lack of attachment is not a virtue. Strictly speaking, non-attachment is renunciation, the wish to leave samsara. Non-hatred is a special virtuous mind such as love or patience that acts as the opponent of hatred, or anger. Non-ignorance is the wisdom that acts as the opponent of self-grasping, the ignorance of the real nature of phenomena.

When any of the three objects appears to the mind of an ordinary being it usually causes one or more of the three mental poisons to develop. Attractive objects cause desirous attachment to arise, unattractive objects cause anger, and neutral objects cause ignorance. For ordinary beings, all experiences outside meditation involve meeting the three objects and developing the three poisons. Those with special interest in training the mind, however, should try to change this and develop the three virtuous minds instead of the three poisons. Whenever we encounter something attractive we should try not to develop attachment for it, but instead cultivate non-attachment; whenever we encounter something unpleasant we should try not to feel aversion or anger, but instead cultivate non-hatred; and whenever we encounter neutral objects we should try not to develop ignorance, but instead recognize their ultimate nature, lack of inherent existence, and thus increase our wisdom. This practice is called 'restraining the doors of the sense powers'.

By continually practising restraining the doors of our sense powers in this way we shall come to know through our own experience that it is a truly effective method for pacifying our mental poisons and increasing our compassion and merit. When we reach the stage where every object causes us to develop virtuous minds, our whole life will become our spiritual practice. More information on the three mental poisons and the three virtuous roots can be found in *Understanding the Mind*.

If we find that our efforts to restrain the doors of the sense powers during the meditation break are not strong enough to overcome powerful attachment or anger, we can try the following method. First we should try to find the delusion. Is it somewhere inside the body? At the heart or in the head? What is its exact nature? After checking carefully we shall discover that the delusion cannot be found – that it has completely disappeared. The same method can be used to overcome ignorance and other delusions.

Our practice in the meditation break assists our practice during the meditation session and vice versa, and the two together help us to attain realizations quickly. However, this practice of subsequent attainment is not easy because we have been familiarizing ourself with the three mental poisons since beginningless time – so much so that these delusions arise naturally, even during our sleep. Therefore, we need to be both patient and determined in our practice.

As practitioners of training the mind we should engage in the practice of taking whenever the three poisons arise in our mind. With strong compassion we should think:

> *All mother beings have this chronic disease of the delusions, just as I have. May their attachment, anger, and ignorance ripen upon me so that they may all be released from the disease of the three mental poisons.*

To remember this,
Train in every activity by words

These two lines from the root text advise us to memorize certain words to recite at appropriate times so as to remind us of our essential practice of exchanging self with others, and especially of our practice of taking and giving. There are many quotations in the scriptures to choose from. For example, in one Sutra, in reference to the life story of the Bodhisattva Norsang, Buddha says:

> You should think as follows: 'May I take on the sufferings of migrators and may my body transform into whatever they find beneficial.'

In *Praise of Supreme Actions Sutra* Buddha says:

> May the infinite sufferings
> Of gods, demi-gods, and humans,
> Yama, animals, and hell beings ripen upon me,
> And may migrators receive all happiness.

In *Guide to the Bodhisattva's Way of Life* Shantideva says:

> Whatever sufferings living beings may have,
> May they ripen solely upon me;

> And by the power of the Bodhisattvas' virtues and aspirations
> May all beings experience happiness.

And in *Eight Verses of Training the Mind* Geshe Langri Tangpa says:

> In short, may I directly and indirectly,
> Offer help and happiness to all my mothers,
> And secretly take upon myself
> All their harm and suffering.

Repeatedly reciting any of these verses during our daily activities will help us to recall our practice of taking and giving throughout the day.

Ultimate Bodhichitta

TRAINING IN ULTIMATE BODHICHITTA

Show the secret to the one who has achieved firmness

Having generated conventional bodhichitta through the previous meditations, we should now train in ultimate bodhichitta by meditating on emptiness with this bodhichitta motivation. Only Mahayana practitioners train in ultimate bodhichitta. Hinayana practitioners meditate on emptiness principally motivated by renunciation, not by bodhichitta. Those who have not yet realized emptiness should engage in this training to gain an initial understanding of emptiness; and those who already have some understanding of emptiness should train further to deepen their experience.

Wisdom realizing emptiness releases the mind from the two obstructions – the obstructions to liberation and the obstructions to omniscience – which are the root of all our problems. Unless we remove these obstructions from our mind we shall remain forever in a deluded and suffering state. By training in emptiness with bodhichitta motivation we shall free our mind from both obstructions and thereby attain full enlightenment. For this reason we would be well advised to spend our whole life improving our experience and understanding of emptiness. Wisdom realizing emptiness is like medicine because it completely removes our suffering; therefore we should take this supreme remedy without fear.

In general, someone wishing to make emptiness their principal practice should first gain experience of the basic practices by meditating on this precious human life, impermanence, actions and their effects, and all the stages of the

Geshe Potowa

path that lead up to conventional bodhichitta. The last of these is particularly important. The line from the root text, 'Show the secret to the one who has achieved firmness', indicates that we should meditate on emptiness only when we have gained a firm understanding and experience of basic Buddhist meditations, especially the meditations on conventional bodhichitta. In this context, the term 'secret' refers to emptiness in general and ultimate bodhichitta in particular, which should be kept secret from those who have no experience of basic Dharma.

If emptiness is explained unskilfully to those with no basic experience of Dharma there is a risk that they might misunderstand the instructions and instead of realizing the correct view of emptiness fall into the mistaken and extreme view of nothingness, thinking that emptiness means that nothing exists. To avoid this danger a skilful Teacher will not reveal emptiness to begin with, but will concentrate on helping the student to develop experience of the more basic teachings to provide a firm foundation for an unmistaken understanding of emptiness later on.

Training in ultimate bodhichitta has two parts:

1 Training in emptiness during the meditation session
2 Training in emptiness during the meditation break

TRAINING IN EMPTINESS DURING THE MEDITATION SESSION

The root text reveals three ways of training in emptiness during the meditation session:

1 Meditating on the emptiness of phenomena
2 Meditating on the emptiness of the mind
3 Meditating on the emptiness of the I

MEDITATING ON THE EMPTINESS OF PHENOMENA

Think that all phenomena are like dreams

In this meditation we take external phenomena as our object and recognize that they completely lack inherent existence, and are dream-like in nature. In *King of Concentration Sutra* Buddha clearly explains the true nature of phenomena:

> In a dream a girl meets a boy and sees that he is dying.
> She is happy to meet him but unhappy to see him dying.
> We should understand that all phenomena are like this.

In the dream described by Buddha the boy is merely an appearance to the mind of the dreaming girl and has no real, independent existence. The girl, however, does not realize that she is dreaming and, because the boy appears to her as real, feels pleasure at seeing him. The boy's approaching death is also a mere appearance and is not inherently existent, but again, because of her ignorance, it seems to her that he is really dying and so she experiences grief. Everyone has this kind of experience in dreams although, because we all have different karma, the things we see in our dreams are different.

All the objects we encounter when we are awake – pleasant, unpleasant, and neutral – are like objects in a dream in that they are actually only appearances to mind and have no independent, or inherent, existence. However, because of our ignorance we assume that they are truly existent. This is why when we see beautiful things we develop desirous attachment for them, and when we see unpleasant things we feel dislike or anger. Thus, although all phenomena are mere appearances to mind, because of our ignorance we take them to be truly existent and develop deluded minds with regard to them.

A clear and profound presentation of emptiness is given by Shantideva in the ninth chapter of *Guide to the Bodhisattva's Way of Life*. This chapter is very profound and should be read carefully and with strong concentration. No clearer explanation of emptiness can be found. In this chapter Shantideva says that we should examine the way in which we cling to an inherently existent body. When we think 'I have a strong, healthy body', we are thinking of a body that is appearing vividly to our mind as distinct from its parts. At such times we are not thinking of our arms, legs, and so on, but of a body that seems to exist separate from its parts, a body that is truly existent.

If our body were truly existent it would have to exist in one of three ways: as one of its parts, as the collection of its parts, or as something other than these two. We should now check to see if it exists in any of these ways. First we should check to see if the body is one of its parts. Clearly this is not the case because the arms are not the body, the legs are not the body, and so on. This is because all these things are parts of the body. If each of these were the body there would be many bodies instead of just one, which is clearly not the case.

The second possibility is that the body is the collection of its parts, but since none of the individual parts is the body, how can the collection itself be the body? The parts of the body are all non-bodies and so the collection of the parts must also be non-body. The collection of the parts of the body is the basis for imputing body; it cannot be the body itself. A more subtle point that requires very careful thought is that the collection of the parts of the body is not the body because it is a part of the body.

The third possibility is that the body exists as something other than its parts or the collection of its parts, perhaps as a separate possessor of its parts. If the body exists in this way, where is it to be found? Whenever we point to the body we point to a part of the body, and not to an object that is separate from the parts of the body but that possesses them. When we look at the body, we see only parts of the body. If there were no parts there would be no body, so there is no body separate from its parts. Therefore, the body does not exist within its parts and it does not exist separate from them. It exists merely as a phenomenon imputed upon its parts.

Even though there is no truly existent body, nevertheless because our mind is confused and apprehends the parts of the body as truly existent, we perceive a truly existent body.

In *Guide to the Bodhisattva's Way of Life* Shantideva gives the analogy of someone walking in the countryside at dusk who, seeing a pile of stones, mistakes it for a person. Similarly, in the darkness of our ignorance we mistakenly apprehend the parts of the body as a truly existent body. Thus, Shantideva says:

> Therefore, there is no body, but out of ignorance
> The thought of 'body' arises;
> Just like [developing] the thought of a person with
> respect to a pile of stones
> Arranged in a particular shape.

If we engage repeatedly in analytical meditation searching in this way for our body we shall lose our normal appearance of our body, and an emptiness will appear instead. This emptiness is the lack of inherent existence of our body. We should focus on this emptiness single-pointedly, holding it with strong mindfulness. This meditation is known as 'close placement of mindfulness of body'.

If the ultimate nature of the body is emptiness, how does the body exist? It exists like something in a dream, as a mere appearance to mind. Since the body does not exist from its own side but is merely an appearance to mind, there is no basis for generating attachment for the body. As Shantideva asks, 'What wise person would develop attachment for dream-like forms?'

We should first try to gain an understanding of the emptiness of our own body and then, on this basis, apply the same method of analysis to other phenomena. When through analytical meditation we understand the emptiness of phenomena other than the body, we place our mind on this emptiness, holding it with mindfulness. This meditation is called 'close placement of mindfulness of phenomena'. These two close placement meditations are referred to in the line from the root text, 'Think that all phenomena are like dreams.'

MEDITATING ON THE EMPTINESS OF THE MIND

Analyze the unborn nature of cognition

Here 'cognition' refers to mind. This line advises us to analyze the nature of the mind. The ultimate nature of the mind is its lack of inherent existence, and this is 'unborn' because it is not produced from causes. To meditate on the emptiness of the mind we can apply the same process of investigation as we do when meditating on the emptiness of the body.

Whether our mind is happy or unhappy we always perceive it as an independent entity that exists without depending upon anything else; but in reality our mind is merely imputed by conceptual thought in dependence upon its own past, present, and future moments. The mind does not exist from its own side. If it did we would be able to find it among its past, present, or future moments; but if we investigate we cannot find the mind either within its own continuum or separate from its continuum. The unfindability of the mind through investigation is a clear indication that it does not exist from its own side.

We should meditate for as long as possible with single-pointed concentration on this emptiness, or lack of inherent existence, of the mind. This meditation is called 'close placement of mindfulness of mind'. In the same way we can examine our feelings and meditate single-pointedly with mindfulness on their lack of inherent existence. This meditation is called 'close placement of mindfulness of feelings'.

The line from the root text, 'Analyze the unborn nature of cognition', refers to both close placement of mindfulness of mind and close placement of mindfulness of feelings. Thus, this and the preceding line together refer to the four close placements of mindfulness observing emptiness. These are explained clearly in the ninth chapter of *Guide to the Bodhisattva's Way of Life*, a commentary to which can be found in *Meaningful to Behold*.

MEDITATING ON THE EMPTINESS OF THE I

Even the opponent oneself is free of existing from its own side

This next line from the root text refers to the meditation on the selflessness of persons. It advises us that through meditation we shall realize clearly that we ourself also lack inherent or independent existence. 'Opponent' here refers to the person who is striving to overcome and eliminate self-grasping.

When through analytical meditation we have understood that the body is empty of inherent existence, we shall also be able to understand that the person or self is empty of inherent existence. As Shantideva says in *Guide to the Bodhisattva's Way of Life*:

> Since no body exists in this way
> How can male and female exist?

As we can see, men and women have different bodies with different distinguishing characteristics, but since there is no inherently existent body how can there be inherently existent men and inherently existent women? If man and woman do not inherently exist, how can there be an inherently existent person or self? These points should be considered carefully again and again. If negative ideas arise and interfere with our contemplation we should not succumb to them but instead bring to mind thoughts that help and support our understanding of emptiness.

Immediately before we think 'I', we perceive one or more of our five aggregates: the aggregates of form, feeling, discrimination, compositional factors, and consciousness. In dependence upon perceiving our aggregates we instantly develop the thought 'I', and we firmly believe this I to be real and inherently existent. However, if we look for this I among the aggregates of our body and mind we cannot find it because neither the body nor the mind is the I.

When we say 'my body' and 'my mind' we conceive an I that is different from our aggregates of body and mind, and yet it is only because we perceive our aggregates that we grasp strongly at an independent I. No matter how long we search for an I existing independently of our body and mind we shall never find one. This non-findability of the I indicates that the I or self is a mere appearance to the mind. In this way we can understand that the I does not exist from its own side.

Place the actual path on the basis of all

The previous four lines of the root text refer to analytical meditation on emptiness, and this line refers to placement meditation on emptiness. In some Sutras and Tantras Buddha uses the term 'basis of all' to denote emptiness. In the *Heart Sutra* it says that all phenomena, such as forms, are manifestations of their emptiness. In this sense emptiness is the basis of all phenomena. Therefore, in the present context 'basis of all' refers to emptiness, the ultimate nature of all phenomena including mind and persons.

If we are meditating on the emptiness of our body, for example, we first use logical reasons to gain a rough understanding of the emptiness of our body and then we take this emptiness as our object of meditation. When through further analytical meditation we perceive emptiness clearly we focus our mind single-pointedly on it and meditate for as long as possible. This is placement meditation on emptiness, and is the actual path to liberation.

To eliminate the two obstructions completely we must attain ultimate bodhichitta – a wisdom, motivated by conventional bodhichitta, that realizes emptiness directly. However, it is not possible to realize emptiness directly without first attaining the mental stabilization of tranquil abiding. To do this we can take a rough understanding of emptiness as our object of meditation and then progress gradually through the nine mental abidings until we attain actual tranquil abiding. By continuing to meditate on emptiness with the mind of tranquil abiding we shall eventually attain superior seeing observing emptiness. Then, by meditating with the union of tranquil abiding and superior seeing observing emptiness, we shall eventually attain a wisdom that realizes emptiness directly. More information on tranquil abiding and superior seeing can be found in *Joyful Path of Good Fortune* and *Meaningful to Behold*.

When we attain the realization of conventional bodhichitta we enter the first of the five Mahayana paths, the path of accumulation; when we attain superior seeing observing emptiness we enter the second Mahayana path, the path of preparation; and when we attain the wisdom that directly realizes emptiness we attain the realization of ultimate bodhichitta and enter the third Mahayana path, the path of seeing. Through further meditation we progress to the fourth Mahayana path, the path of meditation; and after further meditation finally we enter the fifth Mahayana path, the Path of No More Learning, which is the stage of full enlightenment.

TRAINING IN EMPTINESS DURING THE MEDITATION BREAK

Between sessions, consider all phenomena as illusory

During the meditation break we should remember that everything that appears to our mind is empty of inherent existence. Although all phenomena will still appear to us to exist inherently we should remember that they are by nature empty. In this sense we are like a magician who can conjure up an appearance of, say, a horse. Even though a horse appears to his mind he is not taken in by it and does not think that it is a real horse. In the same way, even though, during the meditation break, phenomena still appear to our mind to be inherently existent, we are not taken in by this appearance but remember that in reality they completely lack inherent existence. In this way we consider all phenomena to be illusory.

The depth of our understanding and experience of emptiness during the meditation break will depend upon our experience during the meditation session. If our experience of emptiness during meditation is successful we shall have a correct understanding of emptiness during the meditation break.

Transforming Adverse Conditions into the Path to Enlightenment

In these impure times we encounter many hindrances, and so we need a special method for transforming difficult conditions into causes of spiritual paths that bring pure happiness. If we are not able to transform adverse circumstances into causes of spiritual paths we shall find it extremely difficult to maintain the peaceful mind that is necessary to complete our spiritual practices.

It is not only unpleasant conditions that can hinder or interfere with our spiritual practice. For example, someone may have a deep interest in practising Dharma but through a sudden acquisition of wealth become totally distracted by worldly activities and lose interest in virtuous practices. Such obstacles can be encountered by both individuals and communities. To begin with, a spiritual community may be quite poor, and yet its members may be content with their spiritual practice and live together in peace and harmony. Later however, if the community becomes wealthier, the members may find themselves involved in much work and many distracting activities, and as a result their pure Dharma practice may quickly degenerate.

Just as wealth that is not used to create the causes for spiritual advancement can cause problems, so too can the lack of money or material necessities. Poverty and hardship can bring discouragement and despondency, and can even lead people to give up their Dharma practice altogether.

Because of these dangers we should never allow material considerations to interfere with our practice. We need to transform whatever circumstances we meet, whether good or bad, into the spiritual path by channelling all our actions in a virtuous direction. This practice is extremely important.

Geshe Sharawa

Those who engage in it successfully will never have to experience anxiety or discouragement but will be able to remain calm and peaceful in all circumstances.

There are two ways to transform adverse conditions into the path to enlightenment:

1 Transforming adverse conditions into the path by adopting a special line of thought
2 Transforming adverse conditions into the path through the practice of the preparations

TRANSFORMING ADVERSE CONDITIONS INTO THE PATH BY ADOPTING A SPECIAL LINE OF THOUGHT

When the container and the contents are filled with evil,
Transform adverse conditions into the path to enlightenment.
Apply meditation to whatever circumstances you meet.

Here, 'container' refers to the world and 'contents' to the beings who inhabit it. The line 'When the container and the contents are filled with evil' refers to the world and its inhabitants being filled with the results of negative karma – adverse conditions and suffering. If a country experiences a major disaster which causes great suffering, such as a flood or an earthquake, that country is said to be 'filled' with the results of the negative karma that was accumulated by its inhabitants. The same is true of all bad circumstances in the world. Famine, drought, and so on are all the result of negative actions accumulated collectively by those experiencing these misfortunes. If our family experiences misfortunes, such as the house burning down, or if our long-cherished plans remain unfulfilled, this is due to negative actions we have committed together in the past. If we personally suffer from a serious physical illness, severe mental problems, or great unhappiness, we are said to be 'filled' with the fruits of past negative actions. Similarly, when we experience any loss or decrease in our worldly fortunes we are experiencing the results of our negative karma. This is the time to transform such unhappy events into the spiritual path. In both good and bad circumstances we should apply the appropriate meditations, such as meditation on compassion, bodhichitta, and taking and giving.

There are two ways to transform adverse conditions into the path by adopting a special line of thought:

1 Transforming adverse conditions into the path by means of method
2 Transforming adverse conditions into the path by means of wisdom

TRANSFORMING ADVERSE CONDITIONS INTO THE PATH BY MEANS OF METHOD

To transform adverse conditions by means of method we change our attitude towards adversities by recollecting the teachings on method. For example, if we become sick, poor, friendless, or meet with terrible accidents; if we are ignored, slandered, or physically assualted; if we suffer mental anguish, depression, and so on, we should remember the teachings on karma and immediately recognize that all these difficult situations are the result of our own past negative actions. We should try to learn from adversities and think: 'My experiencing these adverse conditions is a reminder that if I want to be free from the sufferings they bring I must purify the negative actions that I have accumulated. These misfortunes themselves are encouraging me to purify my negativities.' We should then apply one of the methods for purifying negative karma. In this way, instead of causing suffering, adverse conditions become the means of preventing future suffering and increasing our spiritual practice.

We should also remember that all the suffering and adverse conditions we experience occur because we have taken rebirth in samsara, and samsara is the nature of suffering. If we were not in samsara there would be no basis for our experiencing these conditions. Therefore, when sufferings arise we should view them as a lesson on the dangers of saṃsara and encourage ourself to seek liberation. For example, if we are sick we should think: 'Because I have taken rebirth in samsara, I suffer from sickness; therefore I must escape from samsara as soon as possible.' In this way we generate a strong wish to attain liberation. The wish to escape from samsara is renunciation, and when we generate this mind we enter the spiritual path to liberation.

In tropical countries, during the hot season, many people move to cooler areas to escape the heat. Similarly, when we experience the mental or physical sufferings of samsara we should generate the wish to escape from samsara. If we use our suffering to develop and strengthen our renunciation, it becomes a wise counsellor and a cause for spiritual realizations. Thinking in this way will even help us to reduce our pain because our attention will be diverted to positive thoughts. Some practitioners are so skilled at transforming adverse conditions into the path that they hope their suffering will increase so that they can improve their practice.

Only by training in Dharma can we transform our thoughts in such a positive way. When those without experience of Dharma meet some great misfortune all they can do is become sad and depressed, and turn to their friends for comfort. With Dharma wisdom, however, problems and hardships become causes of renunciation and other virtuous minds. In fact, if we did not experience any adverse conditions it is unlikely that we would generate virtuous minds such as renunciation because it is difficult to develop a genuine wish for freedom while we are enjoying an easy and pleasant life.

Adverse conditions can also be used as a way of increasing our compassion for others. When we encounter problems we should think of the countless beings who are experiencing sufferings of every kind, often much more severe than our own, and in this way generate a wish for others to be free from their sufferings. This wish is compassion.

As the strength of our compassion grows it will lead us to want to act to free all beings from suffering. At this point we can do the practice of taking and giving. We begin by visualizing ourself surrounded by countless sick and suffering beings and, with a mind of great compassion, decide to take all their sufferings upon ourself, gladly and willingly. We then engage in the meditation on taking and giving as already explained. This will help us both to improve our great compassion and to prevent our own sickness. Generating the compassionate wish to accept the suffering of others purifies the negative karma that causes our own sickness.

When ordinary Bodhisattvas experience even the slightest suffering, their compassion for living beings grows stronger because they see their own suffering as an example of the sufferings of others. Gods of the form and formless realms find it difficult to feel compassion for beings of the desire realm because they themselves do not experience manifest feelings of suffering. They also find it difficult to develop renunciation for the same reason. Humans are more fortunate than gods because our suffering can cause us to develop both renunciation and great compassion. Furthermore, we can use all unfortunate conditions to cultivate other good qualities such as patience, love, and bodhichitta. As Shantideva says in *Guide to the Bodhisattva's Way of Life*:

> Moreover, suffering has good qualities.
> Because of sorrow, pride is dispelled,
> Compassion arises for those trapped in samsara,
> Evil is shunned, and joy is found in virtue.

A person who sincerely practises transforming adverse conditions into the path will find many good qualities in suffering, and so he or she will always remain calm and undaunted.

TRANSFORMING ADVERSE CONDITIONS INTO THE PATH BY MEANS OF WISDOM

To transform adverse conditions by means of wisdom we recollect our wisdom understanding emptiness. Faced with any situation of suffering or difficulty, we remember that the three spheres – we, who are experiencing the suffering, the experience of suffering itself, and the object or condition causing our suffering – are empty of inherent existence. For example, if we fall ill and experience pain, we recollect that we ourself, our pain, and the illness causing our pain, are all empty of inherent existence. We then focus single-pointedly on emptiness for as long as possible. This practice will increase our wisdom and reduce our suffering and discouragement. Through further meditation eventually we shall attain a direct realization of emptiness and thus completely eliminate the root of all suffering.

Adverse conditions are mere imputations by conceptual minds that label them 'adverse'; they do not exist inherently. When our understanding of this becomes firm, the difficulties we meet will no longer cause anxiety and frustration, or interrupt our practice of Dharma. For example, suppose there are two people who suffer from the same disease. One transforms the affliction into a positive spiritual practice, while the other does not. As a result of his positive attitude the former will remain calm and cheerful all the time, even when in severe pain, and this may even help him to recover from his sickness; but the latter will only become depressed and anxious, and this attitude may worsen his condition. By considering examples such as this we shall be greatly encouraged in our practice of transforming adverse conditions.

TRANSFORMING ADVERSE CONDITIONS INTO THE PATH THROUGH THE PRACTICE OF THE PREPARATIONS

Applying the four preparations is the supreme method

The practice of the four preparations is the supreme method for transforming adverse conditions into the path through actions. The four preparations are:

1 The preparation of accumulating merit
2 The preparation of purifying negativities
3 The preparation of giving food to obstructing spirits
4 The preparation of making offerings to Dharma Protectors

THE PREPARATION OF ACCUMULATING MERIT

Whenever we experience misfortune or sickness we should recognize that this is the result of our negative actions or lack of merit. Since we do not want such experiences in the future we must strive to correct this fault. If our present life could last forever we would not need to worry about the effects of our negative actions; but our life could end at any time – perhaps tomorrow, or even today. Therefore, any misfortune we experience should immediately urge us to engage in practices for accumulating merit. Whenever we engage in such practices we should make offerings to the Buddhas, Bodhisattvas, and other holy beings and request their assistance.

The best method for accumulating merit is to please our Spiritual Guide in both our words and our actions. Another excellent source of merit is to care for and give material assistance to our kind parents. Besides these, there are many other ways of accumulating merit such as saving others' lives, giving to the poor, painting pictures of Deities or making statues of Buddha, listening to Dharma teachings, taking notes or copying texts, giving Dharma advice and teachings, visualizing the forms of Buddha, developing great compassion and bodhichitta, practising taking and giving, making prostrations with faith, respecting others (especially our Teachers and parents), serving others, trying to control our anger, making others happy, maintaining correct views and a good motivation, generating faith in Buddha, Dharma, and Sangha, and rejoicing in others' virtue and its results. We accumulate merit whenever we help others in any way we can. To increase our accumulation of merit we should always dedicate our virtuous actions to the benefit of others.

If we are poor we should not be depressed but make strenuous efforts to gain the true internal wealth of Dharma realizations, since this is the real source of happiness and peace of mind. With a contented mind we shall be happy even without wealth; but if we have a discontented mind we shall be unhappy no matter how rich we may become. It is important to understand that happiness and unhappiness depend upon the mind. When we are faced with an unfortunate situation we should regard this as a wise counsellor and use it as a means of accumulating merit. In this way even poverty can lead us to virtuous paths; but without such an attitude we shall be constantly worried about our lack of resources.

There are many ways in which adverse conditions can encourage us to engage in virtuous actions. For example, the death of a parent or friend may cause us to take an interest in Dharma. When Gampopa was a young man he and his wife were completely devoted to each other. After a few years of marriage, however, she died, and Gampopa was grief-stricken. Faced with the reality of death and impermanence he saw clearly the faults of samsara, and so he sought Dharma Teachers who could teach him how to gain freedom. By following precious Teachers such as Geshe Jayulwa and Milarepa he finally became a realized being. For Gampopa great sorrow became the direct cause of his following a virtuous path. This experience is not unique to Gampopa but could happen to any of us.

Through engaging in the practice of transforming adverse conditions we should be prepared to face difficulties at any time. As explained before, if we were never to experience any problems we would never develop the determination to engage only in virtuous actions.

THE PREPARATION OF PURIFYING NEGATIVITIES

The very manifestation of suffering should remind us of its cause, our own negative actions. Once we understand that our present suffering is the fruit of our own negative karma we shall refrain from committing non-virtuous actions that accumulate further negative karma and bring further suffering in the future; and we shall purify the negative karma that we have already accumulated. We do not know what non-virtuous actions we have committed in the past and so we do not know what suffering lies ahead of us if we fail to practise purification. The more difficult our circumstances, the more encouraged we should feel to practise purification. In this way we shall learn to transform all our difficulties into virtuous paths.

If the roof of our house is leaking and water is dripping through the ceiling we do not sit back and do nothing – we try to find the hole and mend it. Similarly, when we experience suffering we should consider its cause, non-virtuous actions, and apply the remedy, purification. Rather than being preoccupied with the suffering itself, we should apply the solution. This is the preparation of purifying negativities.

The purification of our negative karma will solve our problems and help us to develop spiritual realizations. Strong purification made every day over a long period will completely purify even the heaviest negative karma, less powerful purification will slightly reduce our negativities, and a small amount of purification will prevent the power of the negative actions we have already accumulated from increasing. Therefore, any degree of purification is very beneficial.

The strength of purification depends upon the way in which the four opponent powers are applied. If we apply them strongly and regularly our purification will be powerful, but if we apply them less strongly and less regularly our purification will be less effective.

The four opponent powers are:

1 The power of regret
2 The power of reliance
3 The power of the opponent force
4 The power of promise

THE POWER OF REGRET

If we consider carefully the dangers of negative actions we shall develop sincere regret for having committed them. If we swallow the tiniest drop of poison we are terrified of the possible effect, but our fear of the effect of our past negative actions should be far greater. External poison may cause us to become sick or even die, but it can only harm us in this one life. The internal poison of negative karma, however, will harm us in all our lives to come. Since this poison is already within us we have good reason to be afraid. If by contemplating in this way we generate strong remorse for our previously committed negative actions, this is the power of regret. Sincere regret will prevent us from repeating such negative actions. Without regret we shall not only fail to purify our negative actions but shall be liable to commit them again and again. The more regret we generate for our negative actions, the more powerful our purification will be.

THE POWER OF RELIANCE

There are two main objects of our negative actions: living beings and the Three Jewels. Most of our negative actions are committed against living beings. For example, motivated by attachment, anger, or ignorance we kill, steal, lie, and so forth. Under the influence of these delusions we have also committed negative actions against higher beings such as Buddhas, Bodhisattvas, and our Spiritual Guides. Sometimes, motivated by wrong views, we have created the heavy negative karma of abandoning Dharma, denying the existence of enlightened beings, or developing disrespect for Sangha.

To purify these negative actions we practise the power of reliance. We rely upon the Three Jewels by going for refuge; and we rely upon living beings by generating compassion and bodhichitta. The more powerfully we go for refuge by relying upon the Three Jewels, and the more powerfully we generate compassion regarding all living beings, the more powerful our purification will be.

THE POWER OF THE OPPONENT FORCE

The third opponent power is the actual antidote to negative actions. Any virtuous action performed out of regret for our past negative actions, with the desire to purify them, becomes an antidote to our negative actions, and is the power of the opponent force.

THE POWER OF PROMISE

The fourth opponent power is the promise not to repeat negative actions in the future. Without this promise the application of the four opponent powers is incomplete and past non-virtues cannot be purified. There are many levels at which this opponent power can be applied. There may be some negative actions that we can give up completely, and that we can comfortably promise never to commit again for the rest of this life. There are others, however, that we find more difficult to give up, and so we should promise to abandon these for however long we can – for a few years, one year, a month, or even just a day. When practising general purification we should promise not to perform any negative action at all for at least one day, or longer if possible.

In summary, to engage in the practice of purifying negativities by means of the four opponent powers we should first realize that in this and previous lives we have committed many non-virtuous actions. These actions will cause us much suffering in this life, prevent us from fulfilling our wishes, and throw us into lower realms in future lives. By considering this we shall feel regret and fear for our accumulated negative karma. Then we should visualize all the Buddhas, Bodhisattvas, and other holy beings in the space in front of us and with complete confidence in their power to protect us recite the prayer of going for refuge. We then apply the power of the opponent force by engaging in any virtuous action such as making prostrations or reciting mantras. Finally we should promise not to commit harmful actions again for a certain period of time, and conclude with a dedication: 'Through this virtuous action may all living beings, including myself, be completely freed from negative karma.' If we practise this every day we shall gradually purify all our negative karma.

Meditation alone is not sufficient to attain Dharma realizations, even though we may apply great effort. To create the right conditions for our meditation to succeed we need also to engage in practices for accumulating merit and purifying negativities. In this way our practice will progress quickly.

THE PREPARATION OF GIVING FOOD TO OBSTRUCTING SPIRITS

Our unhappiness and unbalanced minds are often caused by malevolent spirits who destroy peaceful and virtuous states of mind by causing strong delusions such as anger and attachment to arise suddenly. When this happens our mind becomes unclear and we find it very difficult to concentrate on virtuous objects. We may even develop wrong views, which may make us want to give up our Dharma practice and follow incorrect paths. We can also receive physical harm from spirits. Diseases, disputes, conflicts, dangers from fire, earth, or water, and even extremely bad weather can be caused by spirits. Lojong practitioners with experience in the practice of taking and giving can transform all these adverse conditions into the spiritual path and thereby increase their compassion, love, bodhichitta, and correct view of emptiness. These practitioners give food to the spirits while praying: 'Your harmful actions are helping me to practise Lojong, so you are very kind to me. Please accept this food and continue to make things difficult for me.' Those unfamiliar with Lojong practice can give food to the spirits and local guardians, praying 'Please do not be jealous or cause me harm, but help me to complete my Dharma practice.'

When giving food to spirits we can either make the traditional tormas or use any fresh food. Having blessed it with the mantra OM AH HUM, we dedicate our offering to the spirits and place it outside in a high, clean place.

THE PREPARATION OF MAKING OFFERINGS TO DHARMA PROTECTORS

There are two factors that are essential for the success of our Dharma practice: the elimination of obstacles and the accumulation of favourable conditions. To accomplish these we have to rely upon Dharma Protectors.

Some people may think that Dharma Protectors are mere fantasies created by Mahayana Buddhists, but this is incorrect. Dharma Protectors are not different from Buddhas and

Bodhisattvas. There are two principal ways in which Buddhas and Bodhisattvas help living beings: by manifesting in different aspects as Spiritual Guides who lead living beings to enlightenment by teaching them Dharma; and by assuming the form of different Dharma Protectors who remove obstacles and bestow good conditions. For this reason, Buddha Shakyamuni gave explanations in many Sutras and Tantras of the nature and function of different Dharma Protectors, and of the way to rely upon them. One such protector is Mahakala, one of the many Dharma Protector manifestations of the Bodhisattva Avalokiteshvara, and another is Kalarupa, a manifestation of the Bodhisattva Manjushri. Similarly, other Bodhisattvas emanate in different aspects as Dharma Protectors. All Dharma Protectors have promised Buddha to remove adverse conditions that hinder Dharma practitioners and to create favourable circumstances for their practice to succeed. This is their main function. The extent to which we receive help from Dharma Protectors depends upon our faith and the way in which we rely upon them. If we rely upon them purely and with strong faith it is certain that we shall receive their help.

To succeed in our practice of training the mind, or in any spiritual practice, we should make offerings to the Dharma Protectors with great faith, and request them to remove our obstacles and adverse conditions. In particular, we should request that our practice of transforming adverse conditions into the spiritual path will be successful. Receiving the help of Dharma Protectors is very important since we ourself have little power at present to overcome obstacles or to create favourable conditions.

How to Integrate All Our Daily Practices

This brief essential instruction
Should be applied with the five forces

The meaning of these lines of the root text is that we should integrate all our daily Dharma practices into the five forces because this special method will cause our practices to bear fruit. The five forces are: the force of motivation, the force of familiarity, the force of white seed, the force of destruction, and the force of aspirational prayer. There are two times when we should practise the five forces – before death and at the time of death.

APPLYING THE FIVE FORCES BEFORE DEATH

We need to train in the two bodhichittas in conjunction with the five forces by applying the five forces to each specific practice, such as equalizing self and others and exchanging self with others. If we know how to apply the five forces to one of these practices we shall be able to apply them to all the others, and so there now follows an explanation of how to apply the five forces before death to the practice of equalizing self and others.

THE FORCE OF MOTIVATION APPLIED BEFORE DEATH TO THE PRACTICE OF EQUALIZING SELF AND OTHERS

In this context the force of motivation, or intention, means having a strong wish to practise equalizing self and others and making the firm decision: 'From now on I will practise equalizing self and others sincerely and diligently.' If we have such a strong motivation we shall apply powerful and consistent

Geshe Chekhawa

effort in our practice, and as a result we shall definitely attain the realization of equalizing self and others. Anything can be accomplished with effort, even things that previously seemed beyond our imagination. Since effort depends upon motivation, the force of motivation is of utmost importance.

We should try to remember our wish to practise equalizing self and others all the time. For example, when we wake up each day we should make a special resolution: 'I must try to practise equalizing self and others throughout the day.' Then, before we go to sleep at night we should make another strong resolve. Whatever we do depends upon making a decision. For example, if before falling asleep we make a strong decision to wake early we shall do so. Similarly, if before going to sleep we make a strong decision to practise equalizing self and others we shall maintain this intention throughout the night. Then, once again, when we wake we make a fresh determination to maintain the practice throughout the day. This is how to apply the force of motivation to the practice of equalizing self and others.

THE FORCE OF FAMILIARITY APPLIED BEFORE DEATH TO THE PRACTICE OF EQUALIZING SELF AND OTHERS

Applying the force of familiarity to the practice of equalizing self and others means familiarizing our mind with the practice. Having cultivated the force of motivation as explained above, we should practise equalizing self and others repeatedly, both in the meditation session and during the meditation break, until we attain a deep and stable experience. To gain such a realization we need to practise repeatedly the methods for equalizing self and others so as to become well-acquainted with them. This is like learning to dance. To begin with it is difficult to learn the steps and we are rather clumsy, but with regular training we gradually gain familiarity with the steps so that eventually we can perform them naturally and with ease. In a similar way, meditating on equalizing self and others can be difficult at first, but with regular practice we become familiar with it and our experience develops simply and naturally. To gain proficiency in the practice of equalizing self and others, as in all activities, we need both the motivation and familiarity.

THE FORCE OF WHITE SEED APPLIED BEFORE DEATH TO THE PRACTICE OF EQUALIZING SELF AND OTHERS

Here 'white' means virtuous and 'seed' refers to the collection of merit. Just as growing crops depends upon seeds and favourable conditions, so attaining and increasing pure experience of Dharma depends upon a collection of merit. Of the many methods for increasing our collection of merit, one that is particularly important is the daily practice of the six preparations, especially the practice of offering. When we make offerings to the Buddhas and Bodhisattvas we can either visualize the holy beings in front of us or set up a representation of Buddha's form, such as a statue or painting, and regard this as the embodiment of all enlightened beings. Then, in front of the visualized Buddhas and Bodhisattvas or their representations, we can either place actual offerings – pure water, flowers, incense, light, and food – or imagine these substances and mentally offer them, regarding them as completely pure. We can also offer the first portion of whatever we eat or drink to all the Buddhas and Bodhisattvas with the following prayer:

To the Buddha Jewel, supreme Blessed One,
To the Dharma Jewel, supreme Protector,
To the Sangha Jewel, supreme Friends,
To you, most sublime Three Jewels, I make offerings.

After offering in this way, we can enjoy our food and drink.

We can also mentally offer the various enjoyments of this world such as ornamental gardens and parks, beautiful lakes and mountains, flowers, rivers, precious gems, gold and silver, and all kinds of delicious food. We should regard all the things in this world that are enjoyed by living beings as pure, offer them to the enlightened beings, and imagine that they accept them with delight. Another form of offering is the mandala offering, which we should try to make three times a day, incorporating within it everything that we wish to offer.

When making offerings we should remember the kindness of living beings, generate compassion for them, and make the offering to the Buddhas and Bodhisattvas with the request that all living beings may benefit from our action. By practising methods such as offering to all the holy beings with strong faith and giving to living beings with compassion, our collection of merit will increase and our wish to attain the realization of equalizing self and others will be fulfilled naturally. As Buddha said:

> Those who have accumulated sufficient merit
> Can fulfil all their wishes.
> By eliminating the obstacles of the maras
> They will easily attain the goal of holy enlightenment.

THE FORCE OF DESTRUCTION APPLIED BEFORE DEATH TO THE PRACTICE OF EQUALIZING SELF AND OTHERS

To attain any Dharma realizations we must use the force of destruction, which is the application of strong effort to eliminate inner and outer obstacles. Inner obstacles include self-grasping, self-cherishing, laziness, wrong views, and other delusions, as well as the imprints of negative actions we have committed in the past. Outer obstacles include not finding a qualified Teacher, having no opportunity to practise Dharma, having a short life, and lacking the basic necessities for life.

Every realization has its own particular obstacle. For example, lack of faith in our Spiritual Guide prevents us from attaining the realization of relying upon our Spiritual Guide, and grasping our body as permanent prevents us from realizing our body's impermanence. Similarly, our self-cherishing makes it difficult for us to practise equalizing and exchanging self with others, and deeply engrained anger and lack of compassion and love make it difficult for us to develop the realization of bodhichitta. Our strong tendencies to wrong views make it difficult for us to understand emptiness, and our many distractions make it difficult for us to develop pure concentration. To eliminate all these obstacles that disrupt our Dharma practice we need to apply the force of destruction.

In particular, to gain experience of equalizing self and others and to improve this mind we should strive to purify our negative karma and eliminate our self-cherishing.

THE FORCE OF ASPIRATIONAL PRAYER APPLIED BEFORE DEATH TO THE PRACTICE OF EQUALIZING SELF AND OTHERS

We should begin any practice of training the mind by making special prayers to attain the realization of that practice, and we should finish each practice by dedicating the merit we have accumulated to the realization of that practice. For example, if we are going to meditate on equalizing self and others we should make repeated requests to all the enlightened beings to grant us their blessings so that we may attain this specific realization. After completing the meditation we should make a prayer dedicating our merit to attaining the realization of equalizing self and others.

If we practise equalizing self and others together with the five forces we shall definitely attain special realizations. If we understand how to apply the five forces to the practice of equalizing self and others we shall be able to apply them to all our spiritual practices.

To encourage ourself in this practice we should consider the example of the Kadampa Teacher, Geshe Ben Gungyal, who was famous for the constant mindfulness he employed while training his mind. From morning to night he would keep a close watch on his mind, checking to see whether the thoughts that arose were virtuous or non-virtuous. Whenever a negative thought arose he placed a black stone on the ground in front of him, and whenever he generated a positive thought he placed a white stone there. At the end of the day he would add up the stones. If there were more white stones than black he would shake himself vigorously by the hand, offer praises, and address himself as 'Venerable Geshe'; but if there were more black stones he would chastise himself, 'You rogue, you scoundrel, you charlatan! Don't you fear death? How can you be so confident when your mind is so treacherous?' Then he would exact from himself a promise not to allow such negative minds to arise again. If we are serious in our desire to tame our mind and to accomplish something meaningful with our life, we should practise in a similar way.

APPLYING THE FIVE FORCES AT THE TIME OF DEATH

The five forces are the most important practice
Of the instructions on Mahayana transference

These lines of the root text refer to the practice of the five forces at the time of death. They explain that this practice is the essential method of transference of consciousness for Mahayana practitioners. The main practice of Mahayana practitioners is to develop compassion, bodhichitta, and the correct view of emptiness. If Mahayana trainees practise these at the time of death in conjunction with the five forces they will be able to transfer their consciousness to the Pure Land of a Buddha.

THE FORCE OF MOTIVATION APPLIED AT THE TIME OF DEATH

When the time of death comes we need to develop a special motivation in order to determine where we shall take our next rebirth. At that time we should think 'To help and protect other living beings I will take rebirth in a Buddha's Pure Land' or 'I will take a precious human rebirth', or whatever we have decided. Motivated in this way we should hold the mind of compassion and love for others until our last breath. If we practise this sincerely, the power of developing such a special motivation will definitely cause us to be born in the place of our wish. In our next life we shall have a special power to protect others, to generate bodhichitta, and to attain other Mahayana realizations.

THE FORCE OF FAMILIARITY APPLIED AT THE TIME OF DEATH

We should try to transform whatever conditions are causing our death, whether it is an accident or illness, into an opportunity to practise taking and giving, and to generate compassion, love, and wisdom realizing emptiness. When death is imminent, rather than allowing pain and other difficulties to impede our practice we should transform these into causes for increasing our familiarity with virtuous minds such as love and compassion; and we should continue to familiarize ourself with these virtuous minds until our last breath. In this way we shall carry our Lojong practice into our next life without it degenerating.

THE FORCE OF WHITE SEED APPLIED AT THE TIME OF DEATH

Since the time of our death is very uncertain we need to practise many kinds of virtuous action to prepare for our future lives. When the signs of death appear we should make a special effort to increase our collection of merit and to purify our negative karma by engaging in the six preparations and by making offerings to the Buddhas and Bodhisattvas.

When we are approaching death we should not worry about leaving our possessions behind, but should be like people who happily go on holiday without worrying about the things they leave at home. While we still have time we should take the opportunity to accumulate merit by distributing our belongings. We can use our money and possessions to accumulate merit by offering them to spiritual communities and charitable organizations, and by giving to those in need. In this way we shall have no possessions to cling to at the time of death.

Some people have great attachment to their body and are afraid of leaving it. If in addition to all the negative actions we have accumulated we also develop strong attachment to our body at the time of death, we risk taking a very unfortunate rebirth. Once, at the time of Buddha Shakyamuni, a woman's corpse lay on the seashore, and inside its head there lived a big worm. From time to time the worm would emerge from one nostril and crawl back through the other. It would leave the corpse only briefly, not liking to be separated from its home. If people tried to remove it, it always returned. The worm's behaviour puzzled the people and so they asked Buddha to explain it. Buddha explained that the dead woman had committed negative actions which resulted in her taking rebirth as a worm. At the time of her death she was greatly attached to her body and so she took rebirth as a worm inhabiting her old body. Buddha then taught those people about the relationship between actions and their effects, and advised them to abandon attachment to their bodies at the time of death.

The danger of developing attachment at the time of death is also illustrated by the story of a man who lived near my first monastery in Tibet. He had collected some silver coins and, to keep them safe, had hidden them inside a teapot. Later he suffered a stroke which impaired his speech. As he lay dying he kept repeating the word 'teapot' to his companion, who understood him to want a cup of tea and thought no more about it. After the man's death his house was sold and his belongings removed. When the teapot containing his silver coins was discovered the people saw that there was a small snake among the coins. They broke the teapot and tried to remove the snake, but it became very aggressive and strongly resisted being separated from the coins. A great Lama who had clairvoyant powers explained that the snake was the reincarnation of the man who had owned the coins. The person who had been with the dying man then understood his constant requests for the teapot!

Before we die it is important to use our possessions to accumulate merit by making offerings to holy beings and Dharma communities, and to practise generosity towards those in need. We must also try to eliminate all kinds of attachment to material things, particularly our own body. In this way we shall be able to die with a peaceful and virtuous mind. This is how to apply the force of white seed at the time of death.

THE FORCE OF DESTRUCTION APPLIED AT THE TIME OF DEATH

The main obstacles to taking rebirth in a Buddha's Pure Land, such as Keajra, the Pure Land of Vajrayogini, or Sukhavati, the Pure Land of Amitabha, or in the human realm, are negative karma and developing strong delusions at the time of death. Therefore, we must purify our non-virtuous actions before we die, and at the time of death rely upon opponents to prevent strong delusions. It is vital that we prevent strong delusions such as anger, jealousy, or attachment from arising when we are dying; and that we maintain a calm and peaceful mind throughout the death process.

THE FORCE OF ASPIRATIONAL PRAYER APPLIED AT THE TIME OF DEATH

When we recognize signs of imminent death we should make aspirational prayers and dedications to all the Buddhas, Bodhisattvas, and other holy beings. We visualize them in the space in front of us and with great faith repeatedly make the following request:

> *Please grant your blessings so that I may attain a higher rebirth either in a Buddha's Pure Land or in the human realm. There, through continually practising training the mind, may I quickly attain the state of Buddhahood.*

If our actions are always negative there is nothing particularly special about being human because, although we may have a human body, our behaviour is not very different from that of an animal. As Shantideva said, there is no point in someone having a long life if he or she uses it only to commit non-virtuous actions. Such a person fails to realize the meaning of being human. Therefore, when praying to attain a human form, we should pray for a rebirth endowed with the seven attributes of higher lineage: nobility, great beauty, great resources, great power, great wisdom, good health, and long life. If we take rebirth as a human possessing these seven qualities, especially great wisdom, we shall have the best conditions for practising Dharma. If, as we die, we make the aspirational prayer to obtain such a rebirth, and if we remain mindful of this wish throughout the death process, we shall definitely attain another precious human life.

All the innumerable actions we have performed – good, bad, and neutral – have left imprints on our mind. At the time of our death, if we pray to the Buddhas for the fulfilment of our aspirational prayers, imprints left by our virtuous actions will ripen, causing us to be reborn with a precious human life, as a god, or in a Pure Land. Therefore, it is essential to cultivate a positive, virtuous mind at the time of death.

We must prepare for our future lives. Just as we want to be happy throughout our present life, both while we are young and when we grow old, so we should want to be happy throughout all our future lives. The duration of our future lives is far greater than the duration of this present life, and so our future lives are far more important than this life. We cannot assume that our future lives are a long way off; we could find ourself thrown into our next life today. If we could be certain that this life will last for a long time we could afford to be carefree and unconcerned, but every day we hear of people dying unexpectedly of heart attacks or strokes, in car crashes, and so forth. Human life is very uncertain.

Recognizing the importance of our future lives we should apply the five forces at the time of death. Since our ability to do this will depend upon previous experience of Dharma, we should begin now by becoming thoroughly familiar with pure Dharma practice. Then, when the time comes, we shall be able to transform our death into the spiritual path.

Geshe Chilbuwa

The Measurement of Success in Training the Mind

There are six signs of progress in training the mind, which are indicated by the next six lines from the root text.

All Dharma is condensed into one purpose

Dharma has many branches and can be practised on many levels. For example, it can be divided into Hinayana and Mahayana and, within Mahayana, into Sutra and Tantra. Within these general divisions there are many further sub-divisions. Although there are a great number of Dharma practices, all of them have a common purpose – they are all methods for subduing our uncontrolled mind.

Our present mind is like a wild elephant which is out of control and difficult to tame. Governed by this unruly mind we face many difficulties and problems. If we discipline and pacify our wild mind we shall gain control and thereby attain freedom from our present problems. As we begin to control our mind negative thoughts may still arise, but they will have no power over us and will not cause us to commit the negative actions that are the basis of all our problems. With such self-control we shall always be calm and composed, and our mind will remain stable no matter what conditions we encounter. Having gained peace and stability by controlling our mind we can eventually attain the peace of liberation and the ultimate spiritual goal of Buddhahood.

If our practice of training the mind has the effect of making our mind more peaceful and controlled, this is a correct sign that we are meeting with success. On the other hand, if we claim to be practitioners of training the mind but our mind is becoming more and more unruly, this indicates that our practice is incorrect. Effective practice of training the mind requires skill.

Hold to the principal of the two witnesses

The two witnesses are the internal and external signs of progress. If our external actions of body and speech are calm and restrained others may take this as a sign that we are good and sincere practitioners. However, internal signs of progress are far more important, which is why they are referred to in the root text as the 'principal'. The internal signs are that we have controlled and overcome negative minds such as self-cherishing and self-grasping.

It is quite possible to display external signs of having controlled our mind without having any internal signs. To indicate this, Nagarjuna, in *Friendly Letter*, uses the analogy of a mango, which may look ripe from the outside but still be unripe on the inside. Similarly, a person may seem very calm and controlled on the outside but still have an unruly mind. Therefore, outward or visible signs of progress are not sufficient. Our chief concern should be to control our mind.

Always rely upon a happy mind alone

The measurement of having trained our mind is that we are always calm and happy. Before we have trained our mind it changes according to our circumstances. When times are good we are happy, but when they change for the worse we become unhappy. Our mind is so unstable that it can change in an instant, one moment happy and excited and the next downcast and despondent. A controlled mind will remain happy and calm no matter what the conditions. Some scholars and meditators have called training the mind 'the city that is the source of happiness'. There are many cities in the world that claim to offer a wealth of pleasure and amusement, but the only 'city' that provides true, enduring happiness is training the mind. If through our practice of training the mind we maintain a happy mind even when we meet with bad conditions, this is a clear sign that our Lojong practice has been successful.

The indication of having trained is reversal

Here 'reversal' means the complete reversal of our ordinary attitudes. This applies to each of the practices of training the mind. For example, the indication that we have trained well in the preliminary practice of relying upon our Spiritual Guide is reversal of our previous lack of faith; and the indication of success in the meditations on our precious human life and death and impermanence is reversal of our attachment to the pleasures of samsara. Similarly, successful meditation on conventional bodhichitta reverses self-cherishing, and skilful training in ultimate bodhichitta reverses self-grasping ignorance. In summary, the reversal of incorrect attitudes indicates success in the practices of training the mind.

The sign of having trained is possessing five greatnesses

If we succeed in training our mind we shall attain 'greatnesses' or attributes similar to those possessed by five great beings: (1) the great Bodhisattva, (2) the great holder of moral discipline, (3) the great ascetic, (4) the great trainee in virtue, and (5) the great Yogi.

The great Bodhisattva is someone who has attained bodhichitta; the great holder of moral discipline is someone who can observe purely all aspects of moral discipline; the great ascetic is someone who is able to bear all problems and sufferings and transform them into the spiritual path; the great trainee in virtue is someone who finds no difficulty in performing virtuous actions; and the great Yogi is someone who has realized both bodhichitta and the correct view of emptiness.

One is trained if one is able to do the practice even when distracted

This can best be explained by means of the following example. Before training in compassion we may sometimes feel compassion, but at other times we may feel anger or jealousy.

When training in compassion we try to abandon anger, jealousy, and other negative minds, but in unguarded moments we may forget our training, and anger, for example, may suddenly arise. For example, if we are mindfully practising patient acceptance we shall not normally be upset if someone insults us, but if we are so severely provoked that we forget our practice we may well get angry. As we progress further in our practice, however, we shall eventually reach a stage where our compassion is so strong that we never become angry even if we are momentarily distracted. We shall not consciously have to recall our Dharma knowledge if things suddenly become difficult, but shall be able to practise patience and forbearance spontaneously under all circumstances. This is like an experienced rider who does not have to concentrate on staying on his horse – even if his attention wanders he will not fall off. A beginner, on the other hand, must remain constantly aware of what he is doing. Similarly, until we have great experience of compassion we need constant training. We can apply this example of training in compassion and patience to all other practices.

Although we may have completed our formal education, as Dharma practitioners we still have higher qualifications to attain. As we progress in training the mind, each new stage is like gaining a higher qualification. When we enter the path of accumulation we qualify as an ordinary Bodhisattva, when we enter the path of preparation and the path of seeing we gain the second and third spiritual qualifications, and when we enter the fourth path, the path of meditation, we gain the fourth spiritual qualification. Eventually, when we attain the Path of No More Learning, we attain the final qualification of full enlightenment. This indicates that we should advance step by step in training our mind, all the time keeping as our main and final goal the state of great enlightenment.

The Commitments of Training the Mind

THE EIGHTEEN COMMITMENTS

Keeping the eighteen commitments and twenty-two precepts of training the mind is the supreme method for establishing and improving pure moral discipline. Maintaining pure moral discipline is a fundamental practice that is extremely important because it helps us to engage in all the practices of training the mind. It is like a field from which grow all the crops of Lojong realizations such as compassion, bodhichitta, correct view of emptiness, tranquil abiding, and superior seeing. Moreover, maintaining these commitments and precepts is also a profound method for protecting and strengthening our Pratimoksha, Bodhisattva, and Tantric vows.

In brief, the practice of keeping the commitments and precepts of training the mind protects us from following wrong paths and leads us into correct spiritual paths in this and future lives. Therefore, it is extremely important to practise these commitments and precepts with all our daily activities.

Always train in the three general points

This line refers to the first three commitments, called here 'the three general points'. These are:

Do not allow your practice of training the mind to cause inappropriate behaviour
Do not allow your practice of training the mind to contradict your vows
Do not practise training the mind with partiality

Je Tsongkhapa

The first of these points is that no matter how successful our Lojong practice is we should never act inappropriately. When as a result of our practice of training the mind our self-cherishing diminishes slightly we may think that we no longer have self-cherishing and, wanting to prove this, we may engage in unsuitable actions such as abandoning our family, or giving up all our possessions, and even our life, without a good reason. We may expose ourself unnecessarily to risks by visiting dangerous places, deliberately neglecting our body, and so on. This commitment warns us against such recklessness because it will only hinder our spiritual practice. We should always act in a manner that is appropriate to our level of spiritual development.

The second general point is that we should not neglect or disregard any vows we have already taken, such as our refuge, Pratimoksha, Bodhisattva, or Tantric vows, thinking that the practice of Lojong is sufficient to gain a peaceful mind.

The third general point is that we should take all living beings as our object of training the mind, without discrimination or partiality. We should not think 'I will practise love and patience towards my friends and relatives but not towards others', or 'I will try to equalize myself with my friends and those dear to me but not with my enemies', or 'I will practise taking the sufferings of those I love but not those of people I dislike', and so on. This commitment guards us from discriminating in this way.

Remain natural while changing your aspiration

Through the practice of training the mind our ordinary thoughts, attitudes, and aspirations will change; but outwardly we should remain natural with no affectations of body or speech. As we practise Lojong, our tendency to perform negative actions will gradually decrease and our behaviour will change naturally. For example, if an Englishman becomes proficient in training the mind, his way of thinking and his aspirations will be transformed. He will no longer have the thoughts and attitudes of an ordinary Englishman but those of a Bodhisattva. However, there will be no need for him to make any outward changes such as having a special haircut or wearing unusual clothes and ornaments to show that he is a Bodhisattva. When people become ordained they have to change three things – their minds, their name, and their outward appearance – but later when they attain realizations of training the mind no further outward change is necessary.

When Shantideva was at Nalanda Monastery the other monks used to call him 'The Three Realizations' because it appeared that he engaged in only three actions – sleeping, eating, and defecating – whereas he was actually engaged in advanced inner practices of Tantra. During his sleep he would meditate on the yoga of sleeping, so being asleep was more valuable to him than being awake. Thus, although he had great inner realizations, outwardly he appeared quite ordinary. Geshe Chekhawa recommends that we keep our inner qualities such as the attainment of bodhichitta, the realization of emptiness, and clairvoyance hidden from others. In this way we shall experience fewer obstacles to our realizations.

Do not speak about degenerated limbs

This means that we should not point out others' faults without a good reason. The phrase 'degenerated limbs' refers both to physical and mental disabilities such as blindness, deafness, limited mental capacity, and psychological problems; and to the deterioration of spiritual qualities, the degeneration of moral discipline, broken vows, unfulfilled promises, and negative behaviour. This commitment shows that we should not point out others' limitations or faults unless our motivation is pure and we are sure that they will benefit from it. Otherwise we shall only upset them and they will become unhappy and angry.

Constructive criticism can sometimes be beneficial. For example, we have to correct our children when they do something wrong or else they will never learn. In a similar way, if we genuinely want to help someone improve spiritually we may point out their faults. In earlier times a Spiritual Guide would guide his or her disciples by pointing out their faults and showing them which actions and attitudes they needed to abandon. The Teacher had to be faultless for the disciple to be able to accept such criticism. The Kadampa Geshes described the supreme Spiritual Guide as one who exposes his disciples' faults. These days such guidance would upset or infuriate most people.

Usually we can see clearly the shortcomings of others but fail to observe our own, yet it is far more beneficial to examine our own faults than those of others. We all have the basic fault of ignorance. The essential point is to refrain from criticizing others with a bad motivation.

Never think about others' faults

This commitment advises us not to dwell on the faults of others. As conscientious Dharma practitioners we should observe our own shortcomings instead of being preoccupied with those of other people. If we carefully consider our own faults of body, speech, and mind, we shall gain an awareness of them and gradually be able to abandon them. Buddha said: 'A person who is aware of his own faults is indeed wise', and Atisha said: 'Do not look for faults in others, but look for faults in yourself, and purge them like bad blood. Do not contemplate your own good qualities, but contemplate the good qualities of others, and respect everyone as a servant would.' Contemplating our own knowledge and good qualities leads to conceit, but appreciating the good qualities of others leads to virtuous minds such as respect and affection.

Purify your greatest delusion first

If we purify and remove our greatest delusion first, we shall find it easier to abandon other delusions. For example, if we have a tendency towards anger we should concentrate on patience, the opponent to anger, and in this way gradually conquer it. We shall not be able to overcome our anger immediately, but with persistent practice its power will diminish week by week, until eventually it subsides altogether.

If our main problem is desirous attachment we should use specific opponents to reduce its strength. There are several opponents to attachment, such as meditation on impermanence and meditation on the faults of samsaric pleasures. Once we have reduced our desirous attachment we can apply opponents to our other delusions.

If our greatest problem is jealousy we should emphasize overcoming this delusion by meditating on love and compassion, and by rejoicing in the good qualities of others. If all our delusions seem equally powerful we should concentrate on overcoming self-grasping by making meditation on emptiness our main practice. Through this practice all delusions can be abandoned.

Abandon any hope for results

This means that we should not wish for results from our practice for ourself alone. If our main practice is training the mind, our motivation should not be to gain happiness just for ourself, but to help others find happiness and release from suffering. We should dedicate all the merits of our positive actions towards the happiness of others. As a side effect this pure wish for others to be happy will also fulfil our own wish to be happy. This commitment also warns us not to use the practice of Lojong just to achieve worldly goals.

Abandon poisonous food

Here 'poisonous food' refers to virtuous actions that are mixed with self-grasping and self-cherishing. This commitment warns us to avoid contaminating virtuous actions with these minds. Since beginningless time our mind has been constantly under the influence of self-grasping and self-cherishing, even during sleep, and so all our actions have been contaminated. Every practice we do is polluted by these two poisonous attitudes. From a spiritual point of view, therefore, we are like people who eat poisonous food quite unaware of the harm it is causing them. We should understand that mixing virtuous actions with contaminated attitudes is like eating delicious food laced with poison, and make a decision to overcome our self-grasping and self-cherishing by practising training the mind.

Do not follow delusions

This means that we should not tolerate our own delusions such as ignorance, desirous attachment, and anger. Since these constantly destroy our peace of mind and cause us continual suffering they are our real enemy. We need to become fully aware of this and try to avoid falling under their influence. Through force of habit we ordinary beings develop delusions very easily, but if we stop delusions as soon as they arise they will not be so dangerous. For example, we may frequently get angry, but if we drop the anger as soon as it arises instead of holding onto it, its brief appearance will not be very harmful. However, if we indulge our anger and hold onto it for days, weeks, or even years, it will turn into resentment, which is far worse than anger itself. If we have resentment we shall bring great suffering upon both ourself and others. Therefore, as soon as any delusion arises we should immediately let it go. This commitment advises against prolonging negative thoughts that develop easily because of our previous tendencies and familiarity with them.

Do not retaliate to verbal abuse

If someone speaks harshly or spitefully to us, we should not reply with anger or sarcasm. If we do not retaliate it is quite possible that the other person's anger will subside and their mind will become calm. Thus, by practising patience we shall be helping them. By our becoming impatient and answering back, the anger of the other person will increase and this will cause them more harm. There are certain situations in which it is justifiable to reply to harsh words, but never with anger. As a general rule we should not answer back unless there is a very good reason.

Do not wait in ambush

We should not wait for an opportunity to take revenge on our enemies, looking for the best way to hurt them or for the time and place when they will be at their most vulnerable.

Do not offend others

This commitment warns us to avoid speaking or acting in ways that might offend humans, spirits, and other beings. There are many ways of offending others, such as by rejecting their views with a harmful intention, pointing out their mistakes, or refusing to comply with their wishes. As for spirits, we should avoid reciting wrathful mantras or performing wrathful actions with the intention of causing them harm.

Do not transfer your own faults or burdens onto others

We should not pass on our duties and responsibilities to others or try to manipulate others into taking them on against their wishes, even if we find those responsibilities difficult or irksome. There is a saying in Tibetan 'Do not transfer the load of a dzo onto an ox.' A dzo is a strong animal, used in Tibet for carrying very heavy loads. By comparison an ox is much smaller and weaker. This commitment also advises us to avoid blaming others for our own faults but to acknowledge them honestly as our own.

Do not misuse Dharma

Buddha's main intention in expounding Dharma was to help living beings to control their minds and to lead them on the paths to liberation and enlightenment. If we use our knowledge of Dharma to gain wealth, possessions, fame, and control over others for ourself, this is misusing Dharma. There is a danger that we may regard Dharma instructions as we do ordinary education, using them to obtain worldly pleasure, fame, power, a high position, and wealth. It would be sad and shameful if we were to have such a worldly attitude while paying homage to the Buddhas, making offerings and requests, and so on. The very least we can do to repay Buddha's kindness is not to abuse his teachings. Even if we cannot actively practise Dharma, our motives and aspirations should be pure and undistorted. We should develop the motivation: 'I am studying Dharma instructions now so that I may be able to enter the path to liberation in the future. I will use Dharma to subdue my negative mind and to benefit others, both now and in the future.' Without such a motivation it is possible that we shall misuse Dharma teachings.

Do not aim at being the first to get the best

One meaning of this is that if we own something jointly with others we should avoid wanting to possess it all for ourself. Another meaning is that if we share something with others we should not try to take the best parts for ourself. We should also avoid selfish behaviour such as making greedily for the front of a meal queue hoping to get the biggest and best portion, or pushing onto a crowded train or bus to get the best seat.

Do not turn a god into a demon

'God' in this context refers to the practice of training the mind and 'demon' to delusions such as pride and attachment. With correct practice of training the mind all our delusions will diminish, but if we practise in the wrong way there is a danger that our delusions may increase.

Some people have faith in worldly gods as a source of help and protection, but if one of these gods were suddenly to cause them harm it would seem that the god had changed into a demon. The practice of training the mind is a true protector and the supreme method for bringing peace to the mind. However, if we misapply the instructions this may cause our delusions such as pride to increase and destroy our peace of mind, thereby turning this protecting god into a harmful demon. This commitment advises us that all Dharma study and practice in general, and Lojong in particular, should be well understood and applied correctly.

Do not seek happiness by causing unhappiness to others

There are many ways of causing others suffering for the sake of our own personal gain, such as killing, stealing, engaging in sexual misconduct, slandering, and even mistreating employees or deceiving employers. We should try to avoid all of these.

This commitment also advises us not to wish harm on others, for example by hoping that our parents will die soon so that we can inherit their property, or wanting a relationship to end so that we can be with one of the partners, or wishing someone to lose their job so that we can have it for ourself.

In *Guide to the Bodhisattva's Way of Life* Shantideva says:

If I employ others for my own purposes
I shall experience servitude and so forth,
But if I use myself to benefit others
I shall experience exaltation.

It is very difficult to understand how karma functions in detail, but we can know for certain that if we inflict suffering on others to gain happiness for ourself we shall be reborn into a state of servitude with no personal freedom. On the other hand, if we respect others and work for their benefit we shall take rebirth in a powerful family and experience fortunate circumstances.

The Precepts of Training the Mind

THE TWENTY-TWO PRECEPTS

Do all yogas by one

This means that we should perform all our daily activities with the intention of benefiting others. In this context 'yoga' means any action of body, speech, or mind such as eating, drinking, sleeping, rising, working, talking, amusing ourself, studying, praying, or meditating. We should engage in these actions with as pure and virtuous a motivation as possible, preferably with the beneficial intention of wishing to help others. Most of our actions are neutral by nature, but we can make them positive by dedicating them to others.

We can take as an example the yoga of eating. There are three ways of practising this, and we should choose the one that is best suited to our own inclinations. The first, mentioned in the *Vinaya Sutras*, is to regard our food and drink as medicine that cures the sicknesses of hunger and thirst. According to this method, whenever we eat or drink we should do so without attachment, regarding the food and drink as medicine.

The second method, explained in the Mahayana Sutras, is to consume our food and drink with bodhichitta motivation, thinking: 'To help all living beings I need to attain enlightenment. Since my present human body is a perfect basis upon which to attain enlightenment, I must nourish and sustain it.' In this way every action of eating and drinking can be done solely for the benefit of others.

The third way is explained in the Tantras. Out of great compassion for all beings we should generate ourself as a Tantric Buddha such as Heruka or Vajrayogini and, when we

Je Phabongkhapa

are about to eat or drink, transform the food or drink into nectar and regard our eating or drinking it as an offering to ourself generated as the Deity. Another Tantric method is to request all the Buddhas, Bodhisattvas, and other holy beings to appear in the aspect of our own personal Deity, invite them into our heart to merge inseparably with us, and then offer them blessed food and drink.

The yogas of eating explained in the Mahayana Sutras and Tantras are practised with the intention of benefiting others. All Buddhists have a commitment to offer the first mouthful of food and drink to the Three Jewels – Buddha, Dharma, and Sangha. Before we eat or drink we should recite an offering prayer and then apply one of the three methods explained. If we also carry out all our other practices with the intention to benefit others, everything we do will have great meaning.

Perform every suppression of interference by one

Here 'one' refers to the practice of taking and giving. Those who are practising training the mind should rely upon this method for dispelling obstacles such as sickness, powerful delusions, and interference from humans, spirits, and other beings. First we should generate strong compassion, thinking of the countless beings experiencing far greater difficulties than ourself. Then we should make the heartfelt decision to take on all their sufferings, and meditate on taking and giving as described previously. At the end of the meditation we dedicate the action, thinking 'Through the power of my practice of willingly accepting the sufferings of myself and others, may all beings be completely free from suffering.' This is the supreme method for transforming adverse conditions into the path while at the same time improving our own compassion. When we have experience of this practice we shall be able to regard even malevolent spirits with compassion.

There are two activities: one at the beginning and one at the end

Whenever we engage in any spiritual activity – contemplation, meditation, Dharma study, purification of non-virtue, or accumulation of merit – there are two important things to be done: to establish a pure motivation at the outset and to conclude with an appropriate dedication. At the beginning of the practice we should generate a pure motivation and then firmly resolve to carry out that particular virtuous action. After completing the action we should consider whether or not it fulfilled our original intention. If it did, we should feel pleased and dedicate the merits to our attainment of enlightenment. If it did not, we should renew our determination to succeed next time.

In the time between the motivation and the dedication we need to depend upon sharp mindfulness and alertness. Each day, upon rising, we should decide with a pure motivation to perform certain spiritual actions that day. Then until we go to bed in the evening we should use mindfulness and alertness to carry out our decision. At bedtime we should consider how successful we have been. If we have done well we should dedicate joyfully, but if there has been a predominance of negative actions or thoughts during the day we should practise purification. If we do this each day, our spiritual practice will naturally improve and become more and more successful.

Endure both, whichever arises

Here, 'both' refers to the good and bad circumstances that we experience throughout our life. We should accept both kinds of situation and thus prevent either from becoming an obstacle to our spiritual practice. All good and bad circumstances are included among the objects of the eight worldly concerns, or preoccupations: happiness, suffering, wealth, poverty, praise, criticism, good reputation, and bad reputation. These are called 'worldly concerns' because worldly people are constantly concerned with them, wanting some and trying to avoid others. These preoccupations cause difficulties for Dharma practitioners. If we are overly concerned with happiness and suffering, then whenever we experience good fortune we shall become elated and more attached to samsara; and whenever we experience misfortune we shall lose our faith in Dharma. If we are overly concerned with possessing or lacking wealth, then whenever we become rich we shall experience distractions and greater involvement in worldly pursuits to the detriment of our Dharma practice; and whenever we become poor we shall become depressed and worried about material things and, again, our Dharma practice will suffer. If we are overly concerned with receiving praise or blame, then whenever we receive a compliment we shall feel proud and superior to others; and whenever we are criticized we shall suffer badly. If we are overly concerned with a good reputation, then whenever we achieve it we shall ignore our fellow Dharma practitioners and may even feel superior to our Spiritual Guide; and whenever we receive a bad reputation we shall become unhappy. In all cases these eight worldly concerns are obstacles to Dharma practice.

Pure practitioners make use of both good and bad circumstances to develop their spiritual practice, instead of allowing them to impede it. For example, if they are rich they use their wealth to accumulate merit by helping others and, motivated by love, they practise giving extensively. If they are poor they see this as a great opportunity for gaining the inner wealth of moral discipline, concentration, wisdom, and so forth. This helps them to strengthen their practice of taking on the sufferings of others, and to regard the inner riches of spiritual realizations as more important than material wealth. By using their wisdom in this way, practitioners who engage purely in training the mind can overcome the eight worldly concerns and remain content whether they are rich or poor, praised or criticized, respected or held in low repute. Their minds will always remain undisturbed, whatever the circumstances.

Guard both as you would your life

Here 'both' refers to the two sets of commitments: the specific commitments and the general commitments. The specific commitments are the eighteen commitments of training the mind, and the general commitments are all the other commitments we have taken. For Dharma practitioners, commitments are of utmost importance and should be guarded just as carefully as we guard our life. To attain Dharma realizations we need to overcome our faults, and the best way to do this is to keep our commitments purely.

There are two basic commitments for every Buddhist: to go for refuge to Buddha, Dharma, and Sangha, and to abandon harmful thoughts and actions. There are also twelve refuge commitments and many other commitments included in the Pratimoksha, Bodhisattva, and Tantric vows. Those who have taken such vows should keep them very carefully.

Buddha did not give these commitments as punishments. Wise, loving parents want their children to have carefree lives and so they make rules of behaviour that will help them in their everyday life. If the children follow these rules they will usually have few problems and be happy. Parents are generally concerned only for their children's happiness in this life, but Buddha's main wish is for sentient beings to gain freedom from saṃsara and attain the ultimate happiness of enlightenment. Motivated by compassion he explained many practices and gave commitments which, if kept sincerely, will help us to accomplish these goals.

Train in the three difficulties

The 'three difficulties' are three things that we find difficult to do, namely: recognizing our delusions, temporarily pacifying them by applying their opponents, and eradicating them altogether by applying their antidote.

Delusions can be very difficult to recognize. Anger is the most conspicuous delusion, but many other delusions, such as desirous attachment, are quite subtle. Desirous attachment is easily confused with love or compassion. It can also be difficult to differentiate between desire and desirous attachment. Desire is not necessarily a delusion. For example, Buddha has desire to give Dharma teachings and to benefit others, but he has no desirous attachment. Many of our ordinary desires, such as a desire to eat or a desire to meet a friend, are not desirous attachment. A desire is desirous attachment only if it disturbs our peace of mind. We talk of 'falling in love' but often, as this 'love' grows more intense, problems begin to arise. This shows that this 'love' is actually desirous attachment. Real love never creates problems but brings only happiness. This is quite subtle and can be fully understood only through experience.

One of the most subtle delusions, and the most difficult to understand, is self-grasping ignorance. It is virtually impossible to recognize this delusion if we have not trained in Dharma. There are many clever, intelligent people, but they will not understand this deluded mind if they have not studied Dharma. There are two kinds of self-grasping: self-grasping of persons and self-grasping of phenomena. Moreover, self-grasping has many levels from gross to subtle. For example, grasping at a person as being inherently existent is more subtle than grasping at a person as being self-supporting and substantially existent. If we want to understand such distinctions clearly, we definitely need to follow the instructions of a skilled Spiritual Guide. All living beings, even the smallest insects, have self-grasping, but only those who understand it can recognize it as a mistaken awareness. Such understanding can be developed only by studying pure Dharma books and teachings.

If it is difficult to recognize delusions, it is even more difficult to overcome them. We can learn to recognize delusions after having practised Dharma for a while, but it takes much more training to be able to overcome them, and even when we have learned how to subdue them temporarily we still require much more training before we can eradicate them altogether.

The Lojong instructions encourage us to train in these three difficult points. First we need clearly to recognize our delusions; then we need to subdue them temporarily by applying their opponents; and finally we need to eliminate all delusions and their imprints by meditating on emptiness.

Practise the three main causes

There are three main causes that are essential for successful Dharma practice: the wish to practise Dharma, relying upon a Spiritual Guide who teaches Dharma, and having the necessary conditions to practise Dharma. Without these three causes we shall experience many obstacles to our practice.

It is obvious that if we do not wish to practise Dharma we shall not do so. To develop this wish we need to become familiar with the benefits of Dharma, and we need confidence that we are capable of practising it. In everyday life if we see something that we consider useful we automatically want to acquire it. Similarly, if we recognize the advantages to be gained from Dharma practice we shall naturally develop a wish to practise it. Therefore, it is essential to contemplate these benefits.

We also need to find a qualified Spiritual Guide. Without relying upon a Spiritual Guide it is easy to make mistakes but difficult to accomplish the final fruits of Dharma practice. Our Spiritual Guide reveals the meaning of the teachings clearly and faultlessly, shows us how to practise them, and gives support and encouragement in our practice. In this way he or she opens our wisdom eye so that we can look into the mirror of Dharma and follow the path that leads to the state of liberation.

The third of the three main causes is having the necessary internal and external conditions for our Dharma practice. Of the two, internal conditions are the more important. These are strong faith in Dharma and understanding how to practise it correctly and skilfully. The external conditions are adequate food, clothing, and accommodation. For example, those who wish to do a meditation retreat need to have the proper internal qualifications as well as all the special external conditions necessary for their retreat.

Become acquainted with the three non-degenerations

The 'three non-degenerations' are faith in Dharma, effort in our practice of Dharma, and holding mindfully our understanding of the meaning of Dharma. It is essential not to allow these three to degenerate. Rather we should improve each of them day by day, year by year.

If our faith is lost or degenerates we shall give up our intention to practise Dharma. This is the greatest obstacle to gaining inner peace, both temporary and ultimate. Without faith in Dharma, our study and meditation will have no power. Therefore, it is extremely important that we do not allow our faith in Dharma and in our Spiritual Guide to degenerate.

It is also very important not to allow our effort in practising Dharma to decline. If we become lazy we shall never gain any results from our Dharma practice. By applying effort, however, we can accomplish everything we wish.

Thirdly, it is important not to allow our mindfulness to degenerate. We should not forget any of the Dharma knowledge and experience we have gained but should consolidate it and increase it through mindfulness. Mindfulness is the very life of concentration and meditation. If we lose our mindfulness all our Dharma knowledge will be forgotten and our concentration will be lost.

As practitioners of training the mind it is particularly important to improve and enhance our faith in these teachings and in our Spiritual Guide. We should constantly strive in our practice without laziness, and always remain mindful of our Dharma knowledge and experience, particularly of our Lojong practice.

Possess the three inseparables

This precept advises us always to act virtuously with our three doors of body, speech, and mind. These should at all times be inseparable from virtuous actions. Virtuous actions of body include making offerings, making prostrations, helping others, caring for the sick, painting pictures of Buddha, copying Buddha's scriptures, meditating in the sevenfold posture of Buddha Vairochana, and consciously avoiding the non-virtuous actions of body (killing, stealing, and sexual misconduct) having thoroughly understood their dangers. Among the more advanced practices of Secret Mantra, generating our body as the body of a Buddha is also an example of a virtuous action of body.

Virtuous actions of speech include giving Dharma teachings, reciting scriptures, saying mantras, and giving good advice to others. If we sing a pleasing song to make others happy so that they forget their worries, even for a short time, this is also a virtuous verbal action. The supreme verbal action is giving Dharma teachings. By giving Dharma we help others to develop wisdom, and wisdom is the most precious thing we can give. Material wealth, however great, can be enjoyed only for a short time, but if someone possesses wisdom they can call upon it at any time. It brings them benefit not only in this life but also in future lives. Therefore, in the long term giving Dharma instructions is more beneficial than giving material help.

There are countless virtuous actions of mind, such as the eleven virtuous mental factors, faith and so forth; and abandoning the non-virtuous mental actions of covetousness, harmful thoughts, and wrong views.

Train without bias towards the objects

The objects of our practice of training the mind are not only living beings but also inanimate objects such as the four elements and their products. The four elements are earth, water, fire, and wind, and the four products of those elements are forms, smells, tastes, and tactile objects. All of these have various agreeable and disagreeable aspects, and any of them can be objects of training the mind. For example, both pleasant and unpleasant forms can be taken as objects of training the mind. Thus, we should train our mind so that we do not develop aversion towards unpleasant forms or attachment towards pleasant forms.

Conditions that arise in dependence upon the elements and their products, whether good or bad, can also be taken as objects of training the mind. For example, in dependence upon the elements we may experience good conditions such as a beautiful environment where the weather is very comfortable and where diseases are easily cured. We should accept such pleasant conditions while being mindful not to allow ourself to be distracted or disturbed by them. We should not permit favourable conditions to interrupt our practice of Dharma but should remember that these fortunate circumstances are the effects of our previous accumulation of merit, which is now being used up by our present enjoyments and will soon be exhausted. To experience such happiness again in the future we need to accumulate more merit. Knowing this we should strive to engage in further practices for accumulating merit.

Alternatively, we may have the misfortune to live in a place where conditions are poor and uncomfortable, and where there are many dangers such as earthquakes. In this case we should recognize that these unfavourable circumstances are the result of our own past non-virtuous actions and a sign that we need to engage in specific practices to purify our negative karma. Thinking in this way we should strive to practise the methods for purifying negativity.

In addition to applying methods for accumulating merit and purifying negative karma, we should also transform whatever conditions we encounter, whether good or bad, into the spiritual path by practising taking and giving.

It is important to train deeply and encompass all

This precept advises us that it is very important not just to follow the words of Buddha's teachings but also to realize their deeper meaning and thereby to attain profound spiritual experience. It also advises us that in our practice of training the mind we should encompass all phenomena by viewing them all as illusions and empty of existing from their own side.

Kyabje Trijang Rinpoche

Always meditate on special cases

There are special instances that require particular application of training the mind practices. For example, it is often difficult to feel compassion for those whom we consider to be luckier than ourself, or for those who harm or challenge us in some way. In these cases we should meditate specifically on the problems that these people experience and try to develop compassion for them. If there is someone with whom we always seem to get angry we should make a special point of meditating on being patient with them.

During the meditation break we should bear in mind the compassion, patience, and other virtuous minds we generated during our meditation session, and try to put them into practice.

Do not rely upon other conditions

In the practice of training the mind we rely upon our own inner strength rather than upon external conditions. We do not need to wait for better conditions before starting to practise because we can transform any circumstances, whether good or bad, into the path to liberation and enlightenment. If we wait until we find perfect conditions we shall never begin our study and practice of Dharma. Moreover, if we are preoccupied with creating perfect external conditions we shall never find the time to meditate because we shall be too busy trying to fulfil our insatiable desires. For example, we may have a very agreeable partner but because of our discontented mind still look around for someone else, or we may have a good car but still want a bigger and more expensive model. Again, our present job may be very good but out of discontent we still want a better one. If we pursue all our desires there will be little or no time for Dharma practice.

Apply the principal practice at this time

At the moment we have a precious human life, but it is uncertain how long it will last. We should think 'Since it would be a great tragedy to waste this rare opportunity, I must use it in a meaningful way.' It is pointless to work just for material wealth. Even if we were to become very rich we would still have to experience the sufferings of samsara. There are many wealthy people who have great problems and worries. We should think:

> *The greatest purpose of this life is to provide a means for attaining liberation and enlightenment. The only way to attain these is by practising Dharma. Among Dharma practices the supreme practice is training the mind. Therefore, I must practise training the mind now.*

Do not misinterpret

The meaning of this precept is that we should avoid six mistaken attitudes: wrong patience, wrong aspiration, wrong experience, wrong compassion, wrong benefit, and wrong rejoicing.

Wrong patience is patience directed towards inappropriate objects. For example, due to misunderstanding the real meaning of patience we may be impatient with difficulties that arise while we are engaged in virtuous actions but patient with difficulties that occur while we are engaged in non-virtuous actions. True patience is patience with external enemies, not with our internal enemies, the delusions.

Wrong aspiration is aspiration directed towards inappropriate objects. For example, we may admire and wish to emulate those who are rich and powerful and engaged solely in samsaric activities with no wish to follow spiritual practice; but because someone is poor or ugly we may have no wish to be like him, even if he is a pure spiritual practitioner.

Wrong experience is, out of ignorance, putting aside the experience of the nectar of Dharma in favour of following worldly experiences and pleasures. We should try to acquire a real taste for Dharma now while we have the opportunity. As we familiarize ourself with Dharma we shall discover many ways of finding pure happiness. We can experience happiness through meditation and wisdom, and by keeping moral discipline we can attain a special happiness that comes from a healthy body and mind. By enjoying the bliss of pure concentration we can experience supreme and lasting happiness, no matter how difficult our external conditions may be. If, instead of seeking experience of these pure forms of happiness, we seek only the experience of worldly pleasures, this is wrong experience. As Shantideva says in *Guide to the Bodhisattva's Way of Life*:

> Having rejected the supreme joy of sacred Dharma
> That is a boundless source of delight,
> Why am I distracted by the causes of pain?
> Why do I enjoy frivolous amusements and the like?

Wrong compassion is compassion for Buddhas or for other holy beings instead of for suffering sentient beings. Although realized beings may appear to us to be ordinary, they are not suitable objects of our compassion.

Wrong benefit is trying to help others with a good intention but unintentionally causing them more harm than good. It is quite natural to wish to help our friends and relatives, but if our help causes them to commit negative actions any benefit they receive will be only temporary. If a friend wishes to shoot his enemy and we give him a gun this may fulfil his immediate wish but it will certainly cause him suffering in the end. To benefit others effectively we need great skill. At the moment, because of our ignorance, when we try to help others we cannot be sure if we are actually helping or not. We need a wisdom that clearly discriminates between what brings temporary benefit and what brings ultimate benefit.

Wrong rejoicing is rejoicing in others' negative actions rather than in their positive actions. For example, if we applaud someone who catches the most fish in a fishing contest, or someone who shoots the most game at a shoot, or a bull fighter who succeeds in killing the bull, or if we are pleased when an enemy country experiences difficulties and setbacks, these are all examples of wrong rejoicing. Such actions create very heavy negative karma. If, instead, we rejoice in the happiness and good qualities of others, their success, collections of merit and wisdom, and so on, we create very virtuous karma.

Do not be erratic

The effort we apply when practising Dharma should be steady and consistent. If we practise intensely for a few days and then slacken our effort our practice will have little power. Steady, continuous practice over a long period is more important than forceful effort for a short time. Sometimes we practise enthusiastically and energetically for a short time, but when we fail to accomplish results we become discouraged and may even give up our practice altogether. Hoping for quick results in our practice is unlikely to bring success because unreasonable expectations create the cause of failure in any kind of training. We need to practise Dharma with a consistent and enduring effort until we attain enlightenment.

Train with certainty

To gain experience and realizations of training the mind we need to practise wholeheartedly without hesitation or doubt. First we need to understand how to practise by listening to and studying teachings, and then we must practise continuously and steadfastly. A long retreat on training the mind, undertaken with complete dedication, will help greatly in attaining deep realizations of this practice.

Be released by two: investigation and analysis

We should think about all our actions of body, speech, and mind, and check them all carefully. In this way we shall have a precise awareness of what we are thinking, saying, and doing at all times. With such mindfulness we shall avoid inappropriate attention and other deluded minds that induce negative actions of body and speech.

This precept also indicates the two stages of practice in training the mind: rough and precise. The term 'investigation' indicates that through study we should first attain a rough understanding of the meaning of these instructions on training the mind, and the term 'analysis' indicates that we should then gain deep experience of these subjects through contemplation and meditation. In this way we shall be able to free ourself first from gross faults by means of investigation, and then from more subtle faults by means of analysis.

Do not be boastful

If our main practice is training the mind our concern is to help and benefit others, but just because we have such a great purpose we should not become conceited and boast to everyone about what we are doing. Our only reason for practising training the mind is to attain enlightenment for the sake of all living beings. If we are putting ourself at the service of others it is quite inappropriate to boast about it.

Do not get angry

If someone behaves in an unpleasant manner towards us, ridiculing, ignoring, or insulting us, we should not respond with hatred or anger. When we are on the point of getting angry we should immediately recall that the main practice of training the mind is compassion, and that anger is the principal opponent of compassion. By thinking in this way we should try to prevent anger from developing. We should realize that the person who is offending us has no control over what he is doing because he is completely dominated by delusions and so is not free. Usually when those who have not trained their mind see someone hurting another person out of anger, they blame the angry person and think that he or she is in the wrong; but those who practise training the mind blame the person's delusions, not the person. As stated in the Sutras, Buddhas love all living beings because they see that their negative behaviour is the fault of delusions and not of the beings themselves. Buddhas never abandon, condemn, or get angry with living beings but, realizing that they are controlled by their deluded minds, feel only compassion for them. Cultivating the same attitude when someone becomes angry with us is one of the most profound ways of gaining peace for ourself and others.

If all people were to practise training the mind, everyone would love everyone else. Nations would not engage in conflict with each other and so there would be no basis for warfare. Without training in Dharma it is difficult to transform habitual negative actions into positive ones, but wherever pure Dharma thrives such great benefits occur. It seems that for true universal peace and happiness to prevail, Dharma must flourish throughout the world.

Do not be unstable

When some people meet sudden good fortune they overreact and become very excited, laughing and dancing around in an absurd manner; but if their slightest desire is thwarted they become inordinately depressed, downcast, and gloomy, and their whole appearance changes. This precept advises us not to be like this. If we practise training the mind, our mind will remain calm and stable whatever the circumstances.

Do not wish for gratitude

When we help others we should not expect anything in return. Some people think that if they help others they will be rewarded in some way, but this way of thinking turns kindness into a sham. Our actions should be directed solely at the well-being of others, without any thought of gain for ourself. All the practices of training the mind, from the preliminaries through to the final precept, should be done with bodhichitta motivation.

Conclusion

Because of my many wishes,
Having endured suffering and a bad reputation,
I received the instructions for controlling self-grasping.
Now, if I die, I have no regrets.

At the end of the root text Geshe Chekhawa describes his own experience gained through training the mind. The first line reveals why he received the instructions from his Spiritual Guide, the second and third lines explain how he practised training the mind, and the fourth line reveals the results of his practice.

Geshe Chekhawa was given the instructions on training the mind by his Spiritual Guide, Geshe Sharawa, because he had faith and appreciation for the practice as well as a great wish to train in it. During his practice he endured many miseries, criticism, and a bad reputation; and for six years he underwent many hardships and difficulties. He was not concerned with gaining money or a good reputation but practised training the mind by closely following Geshe Sharawa's advice. Through receiving instructions on Lojong and practising them purely he destroyed his self-grasping and self-cherishing and thus gained control over his mind.

Geshe Chekhawa concludes by saying that were he to die now, he would have no regrets. By this he means that he has not wasted his human life. Through his practice of Lojong he purified all his negativities and reached the state of great enlightenment, gaining complete freedom to choose his next rebirth and special power to help living beings extensively.

Geshe Chekhawa's example should greatly encourage us. We should decide to devote all our efforts to generating

Geshe Kelsang Gyatso Rinpoche

bodhichitta and realizing emptiness. These experiences will carry us from joy to joy. We can transform every experience into a cause of Buddhahood by using each moment to develop our realizations of bodhichitta and emptiness. If a blind man finds a piece of gold he will not appreciate its value and may discard it. Now that we have found the gold-like instructions on the two bodhichittas we should not be blinded by our ignorance and confusion into ignoring such a treasure, but should strive from the depths of our heart to realize the most profound meaning of this precious human life.

We are especially fortunate to have the opportunity to study and practise these instructions on training the mind which Geshe Chekhawa taught from his own experience. Any Dharma teaching that is based on authoritative texts, and that is taught by someone who has understood the meaning of the teaching and gained actual realizations of them will be of great benefit to others in the future.

Dedication

Through the virtues I have created by reading, contemplating, and practising these instructions, may all living beings be free from the three mental poisons of attachment, anger, and ignorance, and may they all experience permanent peace.

Appendix I
The Root Text:
Training the Mind in Seven Points

---

by Geshe Chekhawa (1102–1176)
(Headings in bold denote additions made by Je Phabongkhapa)

This text was translated by Venerable Geshe Kelsang Gyatso Rinpoche

The Root Text: Training the Mind in Seven Points

Homage to great compassion.
This essence of nectar-like instruction
Is transmitted from Serlingpa.
It is like a diamond, like the sun, and like a medicinal tree.
The meaning of this text should be known.
The development of the five impurities
Will be transformed into the path to enlightenment.

The preliminary practices of training the mind

First learn the preliminaries.

The main practice: training in the two bodhichittas

Training in conventional bodhichitta

Gather all blame into one.
Meditate on the great kindness of all.
Train alternately in giving and taking.
Begin the sequence by taking from your own side.
Mount these two upon the breath.
The three objects, three poisons, and three virtuous roots
Are the brief instruction for the subsequent attainment.
To remember this,
Train in every activity by words.

Training in ultimate bodhichitta

Show the secret to the one who has achieved firmness.
Think that all phenomena are like dreams.
Analyze the unborn nature of cognition.
Even the opponent oneself is free of existing from its own side.

Place the actual path on the basis of all.
Between sessions, consider all phenomena as illusory.

Transforming adverse conditions into the path to enlightenment

When the container and the contents are filled with evil,
Transform adverse conditions into the path to enlightenment.
Apply meditation to whatever circumstances you meet.
Applying the four preparations is the supreme method.

How to integrate all our daily practices

This brief essential instruction
Should be applied with the five forces.
The five forces are the most important practice
Of the instructions on Mahayana transference.

The measurement of success in training the mind

All Dharma is condensed into one purpose.
Hold to the principal of the two witnesses.
Always rely upon a happy mind alone.
The indication of having trained is reversal.
The sign of having trained is possessing five greatnesses.
One is trained if one is able to do the practice even when distracted.

The commitments of training the mind

Always train in the three general points.
Remain natural while changing your aspiration.
Do not speak about degenerated limbs.
Never think about others' faults.
Purify your greatest delusion first.
Abandon any hope for results.
Abandon poisonous food.
Do not follow delusions.
Do not retaliate to verbal abuse.
Do not wait in ambush.

Do not offend others.
Do not transfer your own faults or burdens onto others.
Do not misuse Dharma.
Do not aim at being the first to get the best.
Do not turn a god into a demon.
Do not seek happiness by causing unhappiness to others.

The precepts of training the mind

Do all yogas by one.
Perform every suppression of interference by one.
There are two activities: one at the beginning and one at the end.
Endure both, whichever arises.
Guard both as you would your life.
Train in the three difficulties.
Practise the three main causes.
Become acquainted with the three non-degenerations.
Possess the three inseparables.
Train without bias towards the objects.
It is important to train deeply and encompass all.
Always meditate on special cases.
Do not rely upon other conditions.
Apply the principal practice at this time.
Do not misinterpret.
Do not be erratic.
Train with certainty.
Be released by two: investigation and analysis.
Do not be boastful.
Do not get angry.
Do not be unstable.
Do not wish for gratitude.

Conclusion

Because of my many wishes,
Having endured suffering and a bad reputation,
I received the instructions for controlling self-grasping.
Now, if I die, I have no regrets.

Appendix II
The Tibetan Script of the Root Text

༄༅། །ཐེག་པ་ཆེན་པོའི་བློ་སྦྱོང་དོན་བདུན་མའི་རྩ་བ་བཞུགས་སོ།།

༄༅། །ཐུགས་རྗེ་ཆེན་པོ་ལ་ཕྱག་འཚལ་ལོ། །ཆོས་ཁྲུངས་བཙུན་པར་བསྟན་པའི་ཕྱིར་མཛད་པ་པོའི་ཆེ་བ་བསྟན་པ། མན་ངག་བདུད་རྩིའི་སྙིང་པོ་འདི། །གསེར་གླིང་པ་ནས་བརྒྱུད་པ་ཡིན། །གདམས་ངག་ལ་གུས་པ་བསྐྱེད་པའི་ཕྱིར་ཆོས་ཀྱི་ཆེ་བ་བསྟན་པ། རྡོ་རྗེ་ཉི་མ་ལྗོན་ཤིང་བཞིན། །གཞུང་དོན་ལ་སོགས་ཤེས་པར་བྱ། །སྙིགས་མ་ལྔ་བོ་བདོ་བ་འདི། །བྱང་ཆུབ་ལམ་དུ་བསྒྱུར་བ་ཡིན། གདམས་པ་དངོས་ཀྱིས་སློབ་མ་ཇི་ལྟར་བཀྲི་བའི་རིམ་པ་ལ་དོན་ཚན་བདུན་གྱི། དང་པོ་སྔོན་འགྲོ་རྟེན་གྱི་ཆོས་བསྟན་པ་ནི། དང་པོ་སྔོན་འགྲོ་དག་ལ་བསླབ། །གཉིས་པ་དངོས་གཞི་བྱང་ཆུབ་ཀྱི་སེམས་སྦྱོང་བ་ལ་དོན་དམ་བྱང་ཆུབ་ཀྱི་སེམས་སྦྱོང་ཚུལ་དང་། ཀུན་རྫོབ་བྱང་ཆུབ་ཀྱི་སེམས་སྦྱོང་ཚུལ་གཉིས་ལས། དོན་དམ་བྱང་ཆུབ་ཀྱི་སེམས་སྦྱོང་ཚུལ་ཡིག་རྙིང་ཐལ་ཆེར་སྔོན་དུ་གསུངས་ཀྱང་། རང་ལུགས་འཇམ་མགོན་ཙོང་ཁ་པ་ཆེན་པོའི་བཞེད་སྲོལ་ལྟར་བློ་སྦྱོང་ཉི་མའི་འོད་ཟེར། བློ་བཟང་དགོངས་རྒྱན། བདུད་རྩིའི་སྙིང་པོ། ཀེའུ་ཚང་རྩ་ཚིག་སོགས་མང་པོར་འོག་ཏུ་གསུངས་པ་བཞིན་དགོངས་པ་ཁྱད་པར་ཅན་གྱི་སླད་འོག་ཏུ་འགོད་པར་བྱ་བས། དེས་ན་ཀུན་རྫོབ་བྱང་ཆུབ་ཀྱི་སེམས་སྦྱོང་བ་ནི། ལེ་ལན་ཐམས་ཅད་གཅིག་ལ་བདའ། །ཀུན་ལ་བཀའ་དྲིན་ཆེ་བར་བསྒོམ། །གཏོང་ལེན་གཉིས་པོ་སྤེལ་མར་སྦྱང་། །ལེན་པའི་གོ་རིམ་རང་ནས་བརྩམས། །དེ་གཉིས་རླུང་ལ་བསྒྲོན་པར་བྱ། །ཡུལ་གསུམ་དུག་གསུམ་དགེ་རྩ་གསུམ། །རྗེས་ཀྱི་མན་ངག་མདོར་བསྡུས་པ། །དེ་ལ་དྲན་པ་བསྐྱུལ་བའི་ཕྱིར།

སྦྱོང་ལམ་ཀུན་ཏུ་ཚིག་གིས་སྦྱང་། དོན་དམ་བྱང་ཆུབ་ཀྱི་སེམས་སྦྱོང་བ་ནི།
བརྟན་པ་ཐོབ་ནས་གསང་བ་བསྟན། །ཆོས་རྣམས་རྨི་ལམ་ལྟ་བུར་བསམ།
།མ་སྐྱེས་རིག་པའི་གཤིས་ལ་དཔྱད། །གཉེན་པོ་ཉིད་ཀྱང་རང་སར་གྲོལ།
།ལམ་གྱི་ངོ་བོ་ཀུན་གཞིའི་ངང་ལ་བཞག །ཐུན་མཚམས་སྒྱུ་མའི་སྐྱེས་བུར་
བྱ། །གསུམ་པ་རྐྱེན་ངན་བྱང་ཆུབ་ཀྱི་ལམ་དུ་བསྒྱུར་བ་ནི། །སྣོད་བཅུད་སྡིག་པས་
གང་བའི་ཚེ། །རྐྱེན་ངན་བྱང་ཆུབ་ལམ་དུ་བསྒྱུར། །འཁྲུལ་ལ་གང་ཐུག་
བསྒོམ་དུ་སྦྱར། །སྦྱོར་བ་བཞི་ལྡན་ཐབས་ཀྱི་མཆོག །བཞི་པ་ཚེ་གཅིག་གི་
ཉམས་ལེན་དྲིལ་ནས་བསྟན་པ་ནི། མན་ངག་སྙིང་པོ་མདོར་བསྡུས་པ། །སྟོབས་
ལྔ་དག་དང་སྦྱར་བར་བྱ། །ཐེག་ཆེན་འཕོ་བའི་གདམས་ངག་ནི། །སྟོབས་
ལྔ་ཉིད་ཡིན་སྤྱོད་ལམ་གཅེས། །ལྔ་པ་བློ་འབྱོངས་པའི་ཚད་བསྟན་པ་ནི། ཆོས་
ཀུན་དགོངས་པ་གཅིག་ཏུ་འདུས། །དཔང་པོ་གཉིས་ཀྱི་གཙོ་བོ་བཟུང་།
།ཡིད་བདེ་འབའ་ཞིག་རྒྱུན་དུ་བསྟེན། །བྱང་བའི་ཚད་ནི་ལོག་པ་ཡིན།
།འབྱོངས་རྟགས་ཆེན་པོ་ལྔ་ལྡན་ཡིན། །ཡེངས་ཀྱང་ཐུབ་ན་འབྱོངས་པ་
ཡིན། །དྲུག་པ་བློ་སྦྱོང་གི་དམ་ཚིག་བསྟན་པ་ནི། སྤྱི་དོན་གསུམ་ལ་རྟག་ཏུ་བསླབ།
།འདུན་པ་བསྒྱུར་ལ་རང་སོར་བཞག །ཡན་ལག་ཉམས་པ་བརྗོད་མི་བྱ།
།གཞན་ཕྱོགས་གང་ཡང་མི་བསམ་མོ། །ཉོན་མོངས་གང་ཆེ་སྔོན་ལ་སྦྱང་།
།འབྲས་བུ་རེ་བ་ཐམས་ཅད་སྤང་། དུག་ཅན་གྱི་ཟས་སྤང་། གཞུང་
བཟང་པོ་མི་བརྟེན། གཤགས་ངན་མི་ཁོད། འཕྲང་མི་སྒུག གནད་ལ་
མི་དབབ། མཛོ་ཁལ་གླང་ལ་མི་བྱོ། །ལྟོ་ལོག་མི་བྱ། འགྲོགས་ཀྱི་རྩེ་

མི་གཏོང་། ལྷ་བདུད་དུ་མི་དབབ། སྐྱིད་ཀྱི་ཡན་ལག་ཏུ་སྡུག་མི་འཚོལ། བདུན་པ་བློ་སྦྱོང་གི་བསླབ་བྱ་བསྟན་པ་ནི། རྣལ་འབྱོར་ཐམས་ཅད་གཅིག་གིས་བྱ། །ལོག་གནོན་ཐམས་ཅད་གཅིག་གིས་བྱ། །ཐོག་མཐའ་གཉིས་ལ་བྱ་བ་གཉིས། །གཉིས་པོ་གང་བྱུང་བཟོད་པར་བྱ། །གཉིས་པོ་སྲོག་དང་བསྡོམས་ལ་བསྲུང་། །དཀའ་བ་གསུམ་ལ་བསླབ་པར་བྱ། །རྒྱུ་ཡི་གཙོ་བོ་རྣམ་གསུམ་བླང་། །ཉམས་པ་མེད་པ་རྣམ་གསུམ་བསྒོམ། །འབྲལ་མེད་གསུམ་དང་ལྡན་པར་བྱ། །ཡུལ་ལ་ཕྱོགས་མེད་དག་ཏུ་སྦྱང་། །ཁྱབ་དང་གཏིང་འབྱོངས་ཀུན་ལ་གཅེས། །བཀོལ་བ་རྣམས་ལ་རྟག་ཏུ་བསྒོམ། །རྐྱེན་གཞན་དག་ལ་ལྟོས་མི་བྱ། །ད་རེས་གཙོ་བོ་ཉམས་སུ་བླང་། །ག་ལོག་མི་བྱ། རེས་འཇོག་མི་བྱ། དོལ་ཆོད་དུ་སྦྱང་། རྟོག་དཔྱོད་གཉིས་ཀྱིས་ཐར་བར་བྱ། །ཡུས་མ་བསྒོམ། ཀ་ལོང་མ་སྡོམ། ཡུད་ཙམ་པ་མི་བྱ། འོར་ཆེ་མི་འདོད། བྱང་ཆུབ་ཀྱི་སེམས་ལ་གདེངས་ཐོབ་པའི་གསུང་གིས་མཇུག་བསྡུ་བ། རང་གི་མོས་པ་མང་བའི་རྒྱུ། །སྡུག་བསྔལ་གཏམ་ངན་ཁྱད་བསད་ནས། །བདག་འཛིན་འདུལ་བའི་གདམས་ངག་ཞུས། །ད་ནི་ཤི་ཡང་མི་འགྱོད་དོ། །དེ་ལྟར་བློ་སྦྱོང་དོན་བདུན་མའི་རྩ་ཚིག་དང་། འགྲེལ་བ་སོགས་བཀའ་གདམས་གསར་རྙིང་གི་གསུང་གི་ཁྲིད་དུ་ཤིན་ཏུ་མང་བ་བཞུགས་ཀྱང་། ཐལ་ཆེར་གཞུང་ཚིག་གི་གོ་རིམ། ཚིག་སྣ་མང་ཉུང་འདྲ་མིན་ཤིན་ཏུ་མང་ཞིང་། འགའ་ཞིག་ཁྲིད་ཀྱི་སྐབས་ཀྱིས་བཅད་ལ་སྦྱར་མ་བདེ་བ་ཡང་ཅི་རིགས། འགའ་ཞིག་ཡོངས་གྲགས་མིན་པའི་རྩ་ཚིག་ཀྱང་སྣ་ཚོགས་སྣང་བ་བཅས་ལ་བརྟེན། རང་ལུགས་འཇམ་མགོན་ཙོང་ཁ་པ་ཆེན་པོའི་གསུང་རྒྱུན་ལྟར་གྱི་བློ་སྦྱོང་ཉི་མའི་འོད་ཟེར། བློ་བཟང་དགོངས་རྒྱན། བདུད་རྩིའི་སྙིང་པོ་རྣམས་ཀྱི

དགོངས་དོན་གསུང་བསྒྲིགས་པའི་རྩ་ཚིག་ཅིག་བྱུང་ན་ཅི་མ་རུང་སྙམ་རིང་ནས་སེམས་སུར། ཞིང་ཕག་ཡོར་ཆབ་མདོ་དགེ་ལྡན་བྱམས་པ་གླིང་དུ་བྱུང་ཆུབ་ལམ་རིམ་ཆེན་མོ་འཆད་སྐབས་གཅིག་ཏུ་སྒྲུབ་པ་ལྷུར་ལེན་ལམ་རིམ་པ་ཕུན་ཚོགས་དཔལ་ལྡན་ནས་ཧེན་བཅས་ཇི་ལྟར་བསྐུལ་བ་བཞིན་རྩ་འགྲེལ་མང་པོར་ཞིབ་བརྟག་གིས་རྩ་ཚིག་ཕྱོགས་བསྒྲིགས་ཕོག། ས་བཅད་ཀྱིས་བརྒྱན་དེ་ཕྱོགས་གཅིག་ཏུ་༢ ཕ་བོང་ཁའི་སྤྲུལ་མིང་པས་བྲིས་པ་འགྲོ་དོན་འཕེལ་བར་གྱུར་ཅིག། ||

Appendix III
The Condensed Meaning of the Commentary

The Condensed Meaning of the Commentary

The instructions on the practice of training the mind have nine parts:

1 The lineage and pre-eminent qualities of these instructions
2 The preliminary practices of training the mind
3 The main practice: training in the two bodhichittas
4 Transforming adverse conditions into the path to enlightenment
5 How to integrate all our daily practices
6 The measurement of success in training the mind
7 The commitments of training the mind
8 The precepts of training the mind
9 Conclusion

The main practice: training in the two bodhichittas has two parts:

1 Training in conventional bodhichitta
2 Training in ultimate bodhichitta

Training in conventional bodhichitta has two parts:

1 The practice in the meditation session
2 The practice in the meditation break

The practice in the meditation session has six parts:

1 Meditating on equalizing self and others
2 Contemplating the dangers of self-cherishing
3 Contemplating the benefits of cherishing others
4 Meditating on exchanging self with others
5 Meditating on taking and giving
6 Meditating on bodhichitta

Meditating on taking and giving has two parts:

1 Taking by means of compassion
2 Giving by means of love

Training in ultimate bodhichitta has two parts:

1 Training in emptiness during the meditation session
2 Training in emptiness during the meditation break

Training in emptiness during the meditation session has three parts:

1 Meditating on the emptiness of phenomena
2 Meditating on the emptiness of the mind
3 Meditating on the emptiness of the I

Transforming adverse conditions into the path to enlightenment has two parts:

1 Transforming adverse conditions into the path by adopting a special line of thought
2 Transforming adverse conditions into the path through the practice of the preparations

Transforming adverse conditions into the path by adopting a special line of thought has two parts:

1 Transforming adverse conditions into the path by means of method
2 Transforming adverse conditions into the path by means of wisdom

Transforming adverse conditions into the path through the practice of the preparations has four parts:

1 The preparation of accumulating merit
2 The preparation of purifying negativities
3 The preparation of giving food to obstructing spirits
4 The preparation of making offerings to Dharma Protectors

How to integrate all our daily practices has two parts:

1 Applying the five forces before death
2 Applying the five forces at the time of death

Applying the five forces before death has five parts:

1 The force of motivation
2 The force of familiarity
3 The force of white seed
4 The force of destruction
5 The force of aspirational prayer

The commitments of training the mind has eighteen parts:

1 Do not allow your practice of training the mind to cause inappropriate behaviour
2 Do not allow your practice of training the mind to contradict your vows
3 Do not practise training the mind with partiality
4 Remain natural while changing your aspiration
5 Do not speak about degenerated limbs
6 Never think about others' faults
7 Purify your greatest delusion first
8 Abandon any hope for results
9 Abandon poisonous food
10 Do not follow delusions
11 Do not retaliate to verbal abuse
12 Do not wait in ambush
13 Do not offend others
14 Do not transfer your own faults or burdens onto others
15 Do not misuse Dharma
16 Do not aim at being the first to get the best
17 Do not turn a god into a demon
18 Do not seek happiness by causing unhappiness to others

The precepts of training the mind has twenty-two parts:

1 Do all yogas by one
2 Perform every suppression of interference by one
3 There are two activities: one at the beginning and one at the end
4 Endure both, whichever arises
5 Guard both as you would your life
6 Train in the three difficulties
7 Practise the three main causes
8 Become acquainted with the three non-degenerations
9 Possess the three inseparables
10 Train without bias towards the objects
11 It is important to train deeply and encompass all
12 Always meditate on special cases
13 Do not rely upon other conditions
14 Apply the principal practice at this time
15 Do not misinterpret
16 Do not be erratic
17 Train with certainty
18 Be released by two: investigation and analysis
19 Do not be boastful
20 Do not get angry
21 Do not be unstable
22 Do not wish for gratitude

Appendix IV
Essence of Good Fortune

Essence of Good Fortune

Mentally purifying the environment

May the whole ground
Become completely pure,
As level as the palm of a hand,
And as smooth as lapis lazuli.

Mentally arranging pure offerings

May all of space be filled
With offerings from gods and men,
Both set out and imagined,
Like offerings of the All Good One.

Visualizing the objects of refuge

In the space in front, on a lion throne, on a cushion of lotus, sun, and moon, sits Buddha Shakyamuni, the essence of all my kind Teachers, surrounded by the assembly of direct and indirect Gurus, Yidams, Buddhas, Bodhisattvas, Hearers, Solitary Conquerors, Heroes, Dakinis, and Dharma Protectors.

Generating the causes of going for refuge

I and all my kind mothers, fearing samsara's torments, turn to Buddha, Dharma, and Saṇgha, the only sources of refuge. From now until enlightenment, to the Three Jewels we go for refuge.

Short prayer of going for refuge

I and all sentient beings, until we achieve enlightenment,
Go for refuge to Buddha, Dharma, and Sangha.
(7x, 100x, etc.)

Generating bodhichitta

Through the virtues I collect by giving and other perfections,
May I become a Buddha for the benefit of all. (3x)

Purifying and receiving blessings

From the hearts of all refuge objects, lights and nectars stream down and dissolve into myself and all living beings, purifying negative karma and obstructions, increasing our lives, our virtues, and Dharma realizations.

Generating the four immeasurables

May everyone be happy,
May everyone be free from misery,
May no one ever be separated from their happiness,
May everyone have equanimity, free from hatred and attachment.

Inviting the Field for Accumulating Merit

You, Protector of all beings,
Great Destroyer of hosts of demons,
Please, O Blessed One, Knower of All,
Come to this place with your retinue.

Prayer of seven limbs

With my body, speech, and mind, humbly I prostrate,
And make offerings both set out and imagined.
I confess my wrong deeds from all time,
And rejoice in the virtues of all.
Please stay until samsara ceases,
And turn the Wheel of Dharma for us.
I dedicate all virtues to great enlightenment.

Offering the mandala

The ground sprinkled with perfume and spread with flowers,
The Great Mountain, four lands, sun and moon,
Seen as a Buddha Land and offered thus,
May all beings enjoy such Pure Lands.

I offer without any sense of loss
The objects that give rise to my attachment, hatred, and confusion,
My friends, enemies, and strangers, our bodies and enjoyments;
Please accept these and bless me to be released directly from the three poisons.

IDAM GURU RATNA MANDALAKAM NIRYATAYAMI

Requests to the Field for Accumulating Merit and the Lamrim lineage Gurus

So now my most kind root Guru,
Please sit on the lotus and moon on my crown
And grant me out of your great kindness,
Your body, speech, and mind's attainments.

Visualize that your root Guru comes to the crown of your head and makes the following requests with you:

I make requests to you, Buddha Shakyamuni,
Whose body comes from countless virtues,
Whose speech fulfils the hopes of mortals,
Whose mind sees clearly all existence.

I make requests to you, Gurus of the lineage of extensive deeds,
Venerable Maitreya, Noble Asanga, Vasubandhu,
And all the other precious Teachers
Who have revealed the path of vastness.

I make requests to you, Gurus of the lineage of profound view,
Venerable Manjushri, Nagarjuna, Chandrakirti,
And all the other precious Teachers
Who have revealed the most profound path.

I make requests to you, Gurus of the lineage of Secret Mantra,
Conqueror Vajradhara, Tilopa, and Naropa,
And all the other precious Teachers
Who have revealed the path of Tantra.

I make requests to you, Gurus of the Old Kadam lineage,
The second Buddha Atisha, Dromtönpa, Geshe Potowa,
And all the other precious Teachers
Who have revealed the union of vast and profound paths.

I make requests to you, Gurus of the New Kadam lineage,
Venerable Tsongkhapa, Jampäl Gyatso, Khädrubje,
And all the other precious Teachers
Who have revealed the union of Sutra and Tantra.

I make requests to you, Venerable Kelsang Gyatso,
Protector of a vast ocean of living beings,
Unequalled Teacher of the paths to liberation and enlightenment,
Who accomplish and explain everything that was revealed
By the Fourth Deliverer of this Fortunate Aeon.

I make requests to you, my kind precious Teacher,
Who care for those with uncontrolled minds
Untamed by all the previous Buddhas,
As if they were fortunate disciples.

Requesting the three great purposes

Please pour down your inspiring blessings upon myself and all my mothers so that we may quickly stop all perverse minds, from disrespect for our kind Teacher to the most subtle dual appearance.

Please pour down your inspiring blessings so that we may quickly generate pure minds, from respect for our kind Teacher to the supreme mind of Union.

Please pour down your inspiring blessings to pacify all outer and inner obstructions. (3x)

Receiving blessings and purifying

From the hearts of all the holy beings, streams of light and nectar flow down, granting blessings and purifying.

Prayer of the Stages of the Path

The path begins with strong reliance
On my kind Teacher, source of all good;
O Bless me with this understanding
To follow him with great devotion.

This human life with all its freedoms,
Extremely rare, with so much meaning;
O Bless me with this understanding
All day and night to seize its essence.

My body, like a water bubble,
Decays and dies so very quickly;
After death come results of karma,
Just like the shadow of a body.

With this firm knowledge and remembrance
Bless me to be extremely cautious,
Always avoiding harmful actions
And gathering abundant virtue.

Samsara's pleasures are deceptive,
Give no contentment, only torment;
So please bless me to strive sincerely
To gain the bliss of perfect freedom.

O Bless me so that from this pure thought
Come mindfulness and greatest caution,
To keep as my essential practice
The doctrine's root, the Pratimoksha.

Just like myself all my kind mothers
Are drowning in samsara's ocean;
O So that I may soon release them,
Bless me to train in bodhichitta.

But I cannot become a Buddha
By this alone without three ethics;
So bless me with the strength to practise
The Bodhisattva's ordination.

By pacifying my distractions
And analyzing perfect meanings,
Bless me to quickly gain the union
Of special insight and quiescence.

When I become a pure container
Through common paths, bless me to enter
The essence practice of good fortune,
The supreme vehicle, Vajrayana.

The two attainments both depend on
My sacred vows and my commitments;
Bless me to understand this clearly
And keep them at the cost of my life.

By constant practice in four sessions,
The way explained by holy Teachers,
O Bless me to gain both the stages,
Which are the essence of the Tantras.

May those who guide me on the good path,
And my companions all have long lives;
Bless me to pacify completely
All obstacles, outer and inner.

May I always find perfect Teachers,
And take delight in holy Dharma,
Accomplish all grounds and paths swiftly,
And gain the state of Vajradhara.

You may do your meditation here or at any appropriate point within the Prayer of the Stages of the Path.

Mantra recitation

After our meditation we contemplate that from the heart of Buddha Shakyamuni, the principal Field of Merit in front of us, infinite light rays emanate, reaching all environments and all beings. These dissolve into light and gradually gather into the Field of Merit. This dissolves into the central figure, Buddha Shakyamuni, who then dissolves into our root Guru at the crown of our head, instantly transforming him into the aspect of Guru Buddha Shakyamuni. He then diminishes in size, enters through our crown, and descends to our heart. His mind and our mind become one nature. We recite the mantra:

OM MUNI MUNI MAHA MUNIYE SÖHA (7x, 100x, etc.)

Dedication prayers

Through the virtues I have collected
By practising the stages of the path,
May all living beings find the opportunity
To practise in the same way.

However many living beings there are
Experiencing mental and physical suffering,
May their suffering cease through the power of my merit,
And may they find everlasting happiness and joy.

May everyone experience
The happiness of humans and gods,
And quickly attain enlightenment,
So that samsara is finally extinguished.

For the benefit of all living beings as extensive as space,
May I attain great wisdom like that of Manjushri,
Great compassion like that of Avalokiteshvara,
Great power like that of Vajrapani.

The Buddhadharma is the supreme medicine
That relieves all mental pain,
So may this precious Dharma Jewel
Pervade all worlds throughout space.

May there arise in the minds of all living beings
Great faith in Buddha, Dharma, and Sangha,
And thus may they always receive
The blessings of the Three Precious Gems.

May there never arise in this world
The miseries of incurable disease, famine, or war,
Or the dangers of earthquakes, fires,
Floods, storms, and so forth.

May all mother beings meet precious Teachers
Who reveal the stages of the path to enlightenment,
And through engaging in this path
May they quickly attain the ultimate peace of full enlightenment.

Through the blessings of the Buddhas and Bodhisattvas,
The truth of actions and their effects,
And the power of my pure superior intention,
May all my prayers be fulfilled.

If we are unable to recite all these prayers for the six preparatory practices in every meditation session, we should at least always remember Guru Buddha Shakyamuni at the crown of our head, recalling that his mind is the synthesis of all Buddha Jewels, his speech the synthesis of all Dharma Jewels, and his body the synthesis of all Sangha Jewels. Then with strong faith we should go for refuge by reciting the short prayer of going for refuge, generate bodhichitta with the words 'Through the virtues . . . for the benefit of all', *offer the mandala, request the three great purposes, and receive blessings and purify.*

If we perform these three practices every time we sit down to meditate – namely, accumulating merit, purifying negative karma, and making requests to receive blessings and inspiration – we shall have accomplished the three purposes of engaging in preparatory practices. At the conclusion of every meditation session we should dedicate our merit.

Colophon: These prayers were composed by Geshe Kelsang Gyatso Rinpoche. The verse of request to Geshe Kelsang was composed by the Dharma Protector Duldzin Dorje Shugdän and included in the prayers at the request of Geshe Kelsang's faithful disciples.

Glossary

Aggregate In general, all functioning things are aggregates because they are an aggregation of their parts. In particular, a person of the desire or form realm has five aggregates: the aggregates of form, feeling, discrimination, compositional factors, and consciousness. A being of the formless realm lacks the aggregate of form but has the other four. A person's form aggregate is their body. The remaining four aggregates are aspects of their mind. See *Heart of Wisdom*.

Alertness A mental factor that is a type of wisdom that examines our activity of body, speech, and mind and knows whether or not faults are developing. See *Understanding the Mind*.

Analysis A mental factor that examines an object to gain an understanding of its subtle nature. See *Understanding the Mind*.

Analytical meditation The mental process of investigating a virtuous object – analyzing its nature, function, characteristics, and other aspects. See *Joyful Path of Good Fortune* and *The Meditation Handbook*.

Aspiration A mental factor that focuses on a desired object and takes an interest in it. See *Understanding the Mind*.

Avalokiteshvara (Tib. Chenrezig) The embodiment of the compassion of all the Buddhas. At the time of Buddha Shakyamuni he manifested as a Bodhisattva disciple. See *Tantric Grounds and Paths*.

Basis of imputation All phenomena are imputed upon their parts, therefore any of the individual parts, or the entire collection of the parts, of any phenomenon is its basis of imputation. A phenomenon is imputed by mind in dependence upon its basis of imputation appearing to that mind. See *Heart of Wisdom* and *Ocean of Nectar*.

Blessing (Tib. jin gyi lab pa) The transformation of our mind from a negative state to a positive state, from an unhappy state to a happy state, or from a state of weakness to a state of strength, through the inspiration of holy beings such as our Spiritual Guide, Buddhas, and Bodhisattvas.

Bodhisattva A person who has generated spontaneous bodhichitta but who has not yet become a Buddha. From the moment a practitioner generates a non-artificial, or spontaneous, bodhichitta he or she becomes a Bodhisattva and enters the first Mahayana path, the path of accumulation. An ordinary Bodhisattva is one who has not realized emptiness directly, and a Superior Bodhisattva is one who has attained a direct realization of emptiness. See *Joyful Path of Good Fortune* and *Meaningful to Behold*.

Buddha A being who has completely abandoned all delusions and their imprints. There are many beings who have become Buddhas in the past, and there are many who will become Buddhas in the future. See *Joyful Path of Good Fortune.*

Buddha nature The root mind of a sentient being, and its ultimate nature. Buddha nature, Buddha lineage, and Buddha seed are synonyms. All sentient beings have Buddha nature and therefore have the potential to attain Buddhahood.

Buddha's bodies A Buddha has four bodies – the Wisdom Truth Body, the Nature Body, the Enjoyment Body, and the Emanation Body. The first is Buddha's omniscient mind; the second is the emptiness, or ultimate nature, of his mind; the third is his subtle Form Body; and the fourth, of which each Buddha manifests a countless number, are gross Form Bodies that are visible to ordinary beings. The Wisdom Truth Body and the Nature Body are both included within the Truth Body, and the Enjoyment Body and the Emanation Body are both included within the Form Body. See *Joyful Path of Good Fortune* and *Ocean of Nectar*.

Buddha Shakyamuni The fourth of one thousand Buddhas who are to appear in this world during this Fortunate Aeon. The first three were Krakuchchanda, Kanakamuni, and Kashyapa. The fifth Buddha will be Maitreya. See *Introduction to Buddhism.*

Collection of merit A virtuous action motivated by bodhichitta that is a main cause of attaining the Form Body of a Buddha. Examples are making offerings and prostrations to holy beings with bodhichitta motivation, and the practice of the perfections of giving, moral discipline, and patience.

Collection of wisdom A virtuous mental action motivated by bodhichitta that is a main cause of attaining the Truth Body of a Buddha. Examples are listening to, contemplating, and meditating on emptiness with bodhichitta motivation.

Concentration A mental factor that makes its primary mind remain on its object single-pointedly. See *Joyful Path of Good Fortune* and *Understanding the Mind*.

Contaminated aggregate Any of the aggregates of form, feeling, discrimination, compositional factors, and consciousness of a samsaric being. See also *Aggregate*. See *Heart of Wisdom*.

Cyclic existence See *Samsara*.

Deity (Skt. Yidam) A Tantric enlightened being.

Delusion A mental factor that arises from inappropriate attention and that functions to make the mind unpeaceful and uncontrolled. There are three main delusions: ignorance, desirous attachment, and anger. From these, all other delusions such as jealousy, pride, and deluded doubt arise. See *Understanding the Mind*.

Delusion-obstructions See *Obstructions to liberation*.

Dharma Buddha's teachings and the inner realizations that are attained in dependence upon them. See *Joyful Path of Good Fortune*.

Dharma Protector A manifestation of a Buddha or Bodhisattva, whose main function is to eliminate obstacles and gather all necessary conditions for pure Dharma practitioners. Also called 'Dharmapala'. See *Heart Jewel*.

Enlightenment Usually the full enlightenment of Buddhahood. There are three levels of enlightenment: small enlightenment, or the enlightenment of a Hearer; middling enlightenment, or the enlightenment of a Solitary Conqueror; and great enlightenment, or the enlightenment of a Buddha. An enlightenment is a liberation and a true cessation. See *Joyful Path of Good Fortune*, *Ocean of Nectar*, and *Clear Light of Bliss*.

Form Body The Enjoyment Body and the Emanation Body of a Buddha.

Form realm The environment of the gods who possess form.

Formless realm The environment of the gods who do not possess form.

Geshe A title given by the Kadampa monasteries to accomplished Buddhist scholars.

Geshe Langri Tangpa (AD 1054-1123) A great Kadampa Geshe who was famous for his realization of exchanging self with others. He composed *Eight Verses of Training the Mind*.

God A being of the god realm. There are many different types of god. Some are desire realm gods, while others are form and formless realm gods.

Ground/Spiritual ground A clear realization that acts as the foundation of many good qualities. A clear realization is a realization held by spontaneous renunciation or bodhichitta. The ten grounds are the realizations of Superior Bodhisattvas. They are: Very Joyful, Stainless, Luminous, Radiant, Difficult to Overcome, Approaching, Gone Afar, Immovable, Good Intelligence, and Cloud of Dharma. See also *Path*. See *Ocean of Nectar* and *Tantric Grounds and Paths*.

Guide to the Bodhisattva's Way of Life A classic Mahayana Buddhist text composed by the great Indian Buddhist Yogi and scholar Shantideva, which presents all the practices of a Bodhisattva from the initial generation of bodhichitta through to the completion of the practice of the six perfections. See *Meaningful to Behold*.

Guru See *Spiritual Guide*.

Heruka A principal Deity of Mother Tantra who is the embodiment of indivisible bliss and emptiness. He has a blue-coloured body, four faces, and twelve arms, and embraces his consort Vajravarahi. See *Essence of Vajrayana*.

Hinayana Sanskrit word for 'Lesser Vehicle'. The Hinayana goal is to attain merely one's own liberation from suffering by completely abandoning delusions. See *Joyful Path of Good Fortune*.

Imprint There are two types of imprint: imprints of actions and imprints of delusions. Every action leaves an imprint on the mind. These imprints are karmic potentialities to experience certain effects in the future. Imprints of delusions remain even after the delusions themselves have been abandoned. They are obstructions to omniscience, and are completely abandoned only by Buddhas.

Imputation, mere According to the Madhyamika-Prasangika school all phenomena are merely imputed by conception in dependence upon their basis of imputation. Therefore they are mere imputation and do not exist from their own side in the least. See *Heart of Wisdom* and *Ocean of Nectar*.

Inherent existence An imagined mode of existence whereby phenomena are held to exist from their own side, independent of other phenomena. In reality all phenomena are empty of inherent existence because they depend upon their parts. See *Heart of Wisdom* and *Ocean of Nectar*.

Inner winds Special winds related to the mind that flow through the channels of our body. Our mind cannot function without these winds. See *Clear Light of Bliss*.

Je Tsongkhapa (AD 1357-1419) An emanation of the Wisdom Buddha Manjushri whose appearance in fourteenth-century Tibet as a monk was predicted by Buddha. He restored the purity of Buddha's doctrine and demonstrated how to practise pure Dharma during degenerate times. His tradition later became known as the 'Gelug', or 'Ganden Tradition'. See *Heart Jewel* and *Great Treasury of Merit*.

Jealousy A deluded mental factor that feels displeasure when observing others' enjoyments, good qualities, or good fortune. See *Understanding the Mind*.

Kadampa A person who sincerely practises Lamrim, and who integrates all the teachings of Buddha that they know into their Lamrim practice. See also *Kadampa Buddhism*.

Kadampa Buddhism 'Kadampa' is a Tibetan word in which 'Ka' means all Buddha's teachings, 'dam' the special arrangement of Lamrim presented by Atisha, and 'pa' a person who practises these teachings. See also *Kadampa* and *Kadampa Tradition*.

Kadampa Tradition The pure tradition of Kadampa Buddhism established by Atisha. Up to the time of Je Tsongkhapa this tradition is known as the 'Old Kadampa Tradition', and after the time of Je Tsongkhapa it is known as the 'New Kadampa Tradition'. See also *Kadampa* and *Kadampa Buddhism*.

Karma Sanskrit word referring to actions. Through the force of intention we perform actions with our body, speech, and mind, and all of these actions produce effects. The effect of virtuous actions is happiness, and the effect of negative actions is suffering. See *Joyful Path of Good Fortune*.

Lamrim Literally, 'stages of the path'. A special arrangement of all Buddha's teachings that is easy to understand and put into practice. It reveals all the stages of the path to enlightenment. See *Joyful Path of Good Fortune* and *The Meditation Handbook*.

Liberation Complete freedom from samsara and its cause, the delusions. See *Joyful Path of Good Fortune*.

Lineage A line of instruction that has been passed down from Teacher to disciple, with each Guru in the line having gained personal experience of the instruction before passing it on to others.

Mahayana Sanskrit word for 'Great Vehicle', the spiritual path to great enlightenment. The Mahayana goal is to attain Buddhahood for the benefit of all sentient beings by completely abandoning delusions and their imprints. See *Joyful Path of Good Fortune* and *Meaningful to Behold*.

Mandala offering An offering of the entire universe visualized as a Pure Land with all the inhabitants as pure beings. See *Guide to Dakini Land*.

Manjushri The embodiment of the wisdom of all the Buddhas. At the time of Buddha Shakyamuni he manifested as a Bodhisattva disciple. See *Great Treasury of Merit* and *Heart Jewel*.

Mantra Literally, 'mind protection'. Mantra protects the mind from ordinary appearances and conceptions. See *Tantric Grounds and Paths*.

Meditation Constant acquaintance of the mind with a virtuous object. There are two types of meditation – analytical meditation and placement meditation. See *Joyful Path of Good Fortune* and *The Meditation Handbook*.

Mental factor A cognizer that principally apprehends a particular attribute of an object. There are fifty-one specific mental factors. See also *Primary mind*. See *Understanding the Mind*.

Merit The good fortune created by virtuous actions. It is the potential power to increase our good qualities and produce happiness.

Method Any spiritual path that functions to ripen our Buddha nature. Training in renunciation, compassion, and bodhichitta are examples of method practices.

Mindfulness A mental factor that functions not to forget the object realized by the primary mind. See *Understanding the Mind* and *Clear Light of Bliss*.

Moral discipline A virtuous mental determination to abandon any fault, or a bodily or verbal action motivated by such a determination. See *Joyful Path of Good Fortune* and *Meaningful to Behold*.

Mundane happiness The limited happiness that can be found within samsara, such as the happiness of humans and gods.

Nagarjuna A great Indian Buddhist scholar and meditation master who revived the Mahayana in the first century AD by bringing to light the teachings on the *Perfection of Wisdom Sutras*. See *Ocean of Nectar*.

Nine mental abidings Nine levels of concentration leading to tranquil abiding. These are: placing the mind, continual placement, replacement, close placement, controlling, pacifying, completely pacifying, single-pointedness, and placement in equipoise. See *Joyful Path of Good Fortune.*

Nirvana See *Liberation.*

Obstructions to liberation Obstructions that prevent the attainment of liberation. All delusions, such as ignorance, attachment, and anger, together with their seeds, are obstructions to liberation. Also called 'delusion-obstructions'. See *Joyful Path of Good Fortune.*

Obstructions to omniscience The imprints of delusions that prevent simultaneous and direct realization of all phenomena. Only Buddhas have overcome these obstructions. See *Joyful Path of Good Fortune.*

Offering to the Spiritual Guide (Tib. *Lama Chöpa*) A special Guru yoga of Je Tsongkhapa in which our Spiritual Guide is visualized in the aspect of Lama Losang Tubwang Dorjechang. The instruction for this practice was revealed by Buddha Manjushri in the *Kadam Emanation Scripture* and written down by the first Panchen Lama. It is an essential preliminary practice for Vajrayana Mahamudra. See *Great Treasury of Merit.*

Path/Spiritual path An exalted awareness conjoined with non-fabricated, or spontaneous, renunciation. Spiritual path, spiritual ground, spiritual vehicle, and exalted awareness are synonyms. See also *Ground.* See *Tantric Grounds and Paths* and *Ocean of Nectar.*

Perfection of Wisdom Sutras Sutras of the second turning of the Wheel of Dharma in which Buddha revealed his final view of the ultimate nature of all phenomena – emptiness of inherent existence. See *Heart of Wisdom* and *Ocean of Nectar.*

Placement meditation Single-pointed concentration on a virtuous object. See *Joyful Path of Good Fortune* and *The Meditation Handbook.*

Pratimoksha Sanskrit word for 'individual liberation'. See *The Bodhisattva Vow.*

Preparatory practices Practices that prepare the mind for successful meditation, such as purifying the mind, accumulating merit, and receiving blessings. See *Joyful Path of Good Fortune* and *The Meditation Handbook.*

Pride A deluded mental factor that, through considering and exaggerating one's own good qualities or possessions, feels arrogant. See *Understanding the Mind.*

Primary mind A cognizer that principally apprehends the mere entity of an object. There are six primary minds: eye consciousness, ear consciousness, nose consciousness, tongue consciousness, body consciousness, and mental consciousness. Each moment of mind comprises a primary mind and various mental factors. A primary mind and its accompanying mental factors are the same entity but have different functions. See *Understanding the Mind.*

Prostration An action of showing respect with body, speech, or mind. See *Joyful Path of Good Fortune* and *The Bodhisattva Vow.*

Puja A ceremony in which offerings and other acts of devotion are performed in front of holy beings.

Pure Land A pure environment in which there are no true sufferings. There are many Pure Lands. For example, Tushita is the Pure Land of Buddha Maitreya; Sukhavati is the Pure Land of Buddha Amitabha; and Dakini Land, or Keajra, is the Pure Land of Buddha Vajrayogini. See *Guide to Dakini Land* and *Heart Jewel.*

Renunciation The wish to be released from samsara. See *Joyful Path of Good Fortune.*

Samsara This can be understood in two ways – as uninterrupted rebirth without freedom or control, or as the aggregates of a being who has taken such a rebirth. There are six realms of samsara. Listed in ascending order according to the type of karma that causes rebirth in them, they are the realms of the hell beings, hungry ghosts, animals, humans, demi-gods, and gods. The first three are lower realms or unhappy migrations, and the second three are higher realms or happy migrations. Although from the point of view of the karma that causes rebirth there, the god realm is the highest realm in samsara, the human realm is said to be the most fortunate realm because it provides the best conditions for attaining liberation and enlightenment. See *Joyful Path of Good Fortune.*

Sangha According to the Vinaya tradition, any community of four or more fully ordained monks or nuns. In general, ordained or lay people who take Bodhisattva vows or Tantric vows can also be said to be Sangha.

Secret Mantra Synonymous with Tantra. Secret Mantra teachings are distinguished from Sutra teachings in that they reveal methods for training the mind by bringing the future result, or Buddhahood, into the present path. Secret Mantra is the supreme path to full enlightenment. The term 'Mantra' indicates that it is Buddha's special instruction for protecting our mind from ordinary appearances and conceptions. Practitioners of Secret Mantra overcome ordinary appearances and conceptions by visualizing their body, environment, enjoyments, and deeds as those of a Buddha. The term 'Secret' indicates that the practices are to be done in private, and that they can be practised only by those who have received a Tantric empowerment. See *Tantric Grounds and Paths.*

Self-grasping A conceptual mind that holds any phenomenon to be inherently existent. The mind of self-grasping gives rise to all other delusions such as anger and attachment. It is the root cause of all suffering and dissatisfaction. See *Heart of Wisdom* and *Ocean of Nectar.*

Sentient being (Tib. sem chän) Any being who possesses a mind that is contaminated by delusions or their imprints. Both 'sentient being' and 'living being' are terms used to distinguish beings whose minds are contaminated by any of the two obstructions from Buddhas, whose minds are completely free from these obstructions.

Shantideva (AD 687-763) A great Indian Buddhist scholar and meditation master. He composed *Guide to the Bodhisattva's Way of Life.* See *Meaningful to Behold.*

Six perfections The perfections of giving, moral discipline, patience, effort, mental stabilization, and wisdom. They are called 'perfections' because they are motivated by bodhichitta. See *Joyful Path of Good Fortune* and *Meaningful to Behold.*

Spiritual Guide (Skt. Guru) Any Teacher who guides us along the spiritual path. See *Joyful Path of Good Fortune* and *Great Treasury of Merit.*

Stages of the path See *Lamrim.*

Superior being (Skt. Arya) A being who has a direct realization of emptiness. There are Hinayana Superiors and Mahayana Superiors.

Superior seeing A special wisdom that sees its object clearly, and that is maintained by tranquil abiding and the special suppleness that is induced by investigation. See *Joyful Path of Good Fortune.*

Supramundane happiness The pure happiness of liberation and enlightenment.

Supreme Emanation Body A special Emanation Body displaying the thirty-two major signs and eighty minor indications that can be seen by ordinary beings only if they have very pure karma. See also *Buddha's bodies.*

Sutra The teachings of Buddha that are open to everyone to practise without the need for empowerment. These include Buddha's teachings of the three turnings of the Wheel of Dharma.

Tantra See *Secret Mantra*.

Three Jewels The three objects of ultimate refuge: Buddha Jewel, Dharma Jewel, and Sangha Jewel. They are called 'Jewels' because they are both rare and precious. See *Joyful Path of Good Fortune*.

Tranquil abiding A concentration that possesses the special bliss of physical and mental suppleness that is attained in dependence upon completing the nine mental abidings. See *Joyful Path of Good Fortune* and *Meaningful to Behold*.

Transference of consciousness A practice for transferring the consciousness to a Pure Land at the time of death. See *Great Treasury of Merit*.

Truth Body See *Buddha's bodies*.

Two obstructions See *Obstructions to liberation* and *Obstructions to omniscience*.

Ultimate truth The ultimate nature of all phenomena, emptiness. See *Heart of Wisdom, Meaningful to Behold*, and *Ocean of Nectar*.

Vajrayana The Secret Mantra vehicle. See *Tantric Grounds and Paths*.

Vajrayogini A female Highest Yoga Tantra Deity who is the embodiment of indivisible bliss and emptiness. She is the same nature as Heruka. See *Guide to Dakini Land*.

Vinaya Sutras Sutras in which Buddha principally explains the practice of moral discipline, and in particular the Pratimoksha moral discipline.

Vows Promises to refrain from certain actions. The three sets of vows are the Pratimoksha vows of individual liberation, the Bodhisattva vows, and the Secret Mantra vows. See *The Bodhisattva Vow* and *Tantric Grounds and Paths*.

Wheel of Dharma Buddha gave his teachings in three main phases, which are known as 'the three turnings of the Wheel of Dharma'. During the first Wheel he taught the four noble truths, during the second he taught the *Perfection of Wisdom Sutras* and revealed the view of the Madhyamika-Prasangika, and during the third he taught the Chittamatra view. These teachings were given according to the inclinations and dispositions of his disciples. Buddha's final view is that of the second Wheel. Dharma is compared to the precious wheel, one of the possessions of a chakravatin king. This wheel transports the king across great distances in a very short time, and it is said that wherever the precious wheel travels the king reigns. In a similar way, when Buddha revealed the path to enlightenment he was said to have turned the Wheel of Dharma because wherever these teachings are present deluded minds are brought under control.

Winds See *Inner winds.*

Wisdom A virtuous, intelligent mind that makes its primary mind realize its object thoroughly. A wisdom is a spiritual path that functions to release our mind from delusions or their imprints. An example of wisdom is the correct view of emptiness. See *Heart of Wisdom* and *Understanding the Mind.*

Wrong view An intellectually-formed wrong awareness that denies the existence of an object that it is necessary to understand to attain liberation or enlightenment – for example, denying the existence of enlightened beings, karma, or rebirth. See *Joyful Path of Good Fortune.*

Yoga A term used for various spiritual practices that entail maintaining a special view, such as Guru yoga and the yogas of eating, sleeping, dreaming, and waking. 'Yoga' also refers to union, such as the union of tranquil abiding and superior seeing. See *Guide to Dakini Land.*

Yogi or Yogini The Sanskrit word 'Yogi' usually refers to someone who has attained the union of tranquil abiding and superior seeing.

Bibliography

Geshe Kelsang Gyatso is a highly respected meditation master and scholar of the Mahayana Buddhist tradition founded by Je Tsongkhapa. Since arriving in the UK in 1977, Geshe Kelsang has worked tirelessly to establish pure Buddhadharma throughout the world. Over this period he has given extensive teachings on the major scriptures of the Mahayana. These teachings are currently being published and provide a comprehensive presentation of the essential Sutra and Tantra practices of Mahayana Buddhism.

Books in print

The Bodhisattva Vow. The essential practices of Mahayana Buddhism. (2nd. edn. Tharpa, 1995.)

Buddhism in the Tibetan Tradition. A guide to Tibetan Buddhism. (2nd. edn. Penguin, 1990.)

Clear Light of Bliss. The practice of Mahamudra in Vajrayana Buddhism. (2nd. edn. Tharpa, 1992.)

Great Treasury of Merit. The practice of relying upon a Spiritual Guide. (Tharpa, 1992.)

Guide to Dakini Land. The Highest Yoga Tantra practice of Buddha Vajrayogini. (2nd. edn. Tharpa, 1996.)

Heart Jewel. The essential practices of Kadampa Buddhism. (2nd. edn. Tharpa, 1997.)

Heart of Wisdom. The essential wisdom teachings of Buddha. (3rd. edn. Tharpa, 1996.)

Introduction to Buddhism. An explanation of the Buddhist way of life. (Rev. 1st. edn. Tharpa, 1995.)

Joyful Path of Good Fortune. The Buddhist path to enlightenment. (2nd. edn. Tharpa, 1996.)

Meaningful to Behold. The Bodhisattva's way of life. (4th. edn. Tharpa, 1994.)

The Meditation Handbook. A practical guide to Buddhist meditation. (3rd. edn. Tharpa, 1995.)

Ocean of Nectar. Wisdom and compassion in Mahayana Buddhism. (Tharpa, 1995.)

Tantric Grounds and Paths. How to enter, progress on, and complete the Vajrayana path. (Tharpa, 1994.)
Understanding the Mind. An explanation of the nature and functions of the mind. (Tharpa, 1993.)
Universal Compassion. Transforming your life through love and compassion. (3rd. edn. Tharpa, 1997.)

Sadhanas

Geshe Kelsang has also supervised the translation of a collection of essential sadhanas, or prayer booklets. Those in print include:

Assembly of Good Fortune. The tsog offering for Heruka body mandala.
Avalokiteshvara Sadhana. Prayers and requests to the Buddha of compassion.
The Bodhisattva's Confession of Moral Downfalls. The purification practice of the *Mahayana Sutra of the Three Superior Heaps*.
Condensed Essence of Vajrayana. Condensed Heruka body mandala self-generation sadhana.
Dakini Yoga: Vajrayogini Six-Session Sadhana. Six-session Guru yoga combined with self-generation as Vajrayogini.
Drop of Essential Nectar. A special fasting and purification practice in conjunction with Eleven-faced Avalokiteshvara.
Essence of Good Fortune. Prayers for the six preparatory practices for meditation on the stages of the path to enlightenment.
Essence of Vajrayana (1). The condensed meaning of Vajrayana Mahamudra and prayers of request to the lineage Gurus.
Essence of Vajrayana (2). Heruka body mandala self-generation sadhana according to the system of Mahasiddha Ghantapa.
Feast of Great Bliss. Vajrayogini self-initiation sadhana.
Great Compassionate Mother. The sadhana of Arya Tara.
Great Liberation of the Father. Preliminary prayers for Mahamudra meditation in conjunction with Heruka practice.
Great Liberation of the Mother. Preliminary prayers for Mahamudra meditation in conjunction with Vajrayogini practice.
The Great Mother. A method to overcome hindrances and obstacles by reciting the *Essence of Wisdom Sutra* (the *Heart Sutra*).
Heart Jewel. The Guru yoga of Je Tsongkhapa combined with the condensed sadhana of his Dharma Protector.
The Hundreds of Deities of the Joyful Land. The Guru yoga of Je Tsongkhapa.
The Kadampa Way of Life. Essential practices of the New Kadampa Tradition.
Liberation from Sorrow. Praises and requests to the Twenty-one Taras.

Medicine Guru Sadhana. The method for making requests to the Assembly of Seven Medicine Buddhas.

Meditation and Recitation of Solitary Vajrasattva.

Melodious Drum Victorious in all Directions. The extensive fulfilling and restoring ritual of the Dharma Protector, the great king Dorje Shugdän, in conjunction with Mahakala, Kalarupa, Kalindewi, and other Dharma Protectors.

Offering to the Spiritual Guide (Lama Chöpa). A special Guru yoga practice of Je Tsongkhapa's tradition.

Prayers for Meditation. Brief preparatory prayers for meditation.

A Pure Life. The practice of taking and keeping the eight Mahayana precepts.

The Quick Path. A condensed practice of Heruka Five Deities according to Master Ghantapa's tradition.

Treasury of Wisdom. The sadhana of Venerable Manjushri.

Quick Path to Great Bliss. Vajrayogini self-generation sadhana.

Wishfulfilling Jewel. The Guru yoga of Je Tsongkhapa combined with the sadhana of his Dharma Protector.

The Yoga of Buddha Amitayus. A special method for increasing life span, wisdom, and merit.

For a catalogue of all our publications please contact:

Tharpa Publications
Kilnwick Percy Hall
Pocklington
York YO4 2UF
England

Tel: 01759-306446
Fax: 01759-306397

E-mail: tharpa@rmplc.co.uk
Website: http://www.luna.co.uk/~tharpa

Study Programmes

Geshe Kelsang has prepared three study programmes based on his books: the General Programme, the Foundation Programme, and the Teacher Training Programme. These are designed to fulfil the wishes of those who would like to study Buddhism systematically and thereby deepen their experience of the essential practices.

The **General Programme** provides a basic introduction to Buddhist view, meditation, and action, and various kinds of teaching and practice from both Sutra and Tantra.

The **Foundation Programme** is designed for those who prefer a more structured approach to their spiritual training. Based on five of Geshe Kelsang's books, this programme lasts for approximately four years. The classes consist of readings, teachings, discussion, pujas, and meditations. Each subject concludes with an examination.

The **Teacher Training Programme** is designed for those who wish to train as authentic Dharma Teachers. This programme, which takes approximately seven years to complete, is based on twelve of Geshe Kelsang's books. To qualify as Dharma Teachers, participants must complete the study of all twelve texts, pass an examination in each subject, satisfy certain criteria with regard to behaviour and life style, and complete various meditation retreats.

These three programmes are taught worldwide at Centres of the New Kadampa Tradition. All these Centres are under the spiritual direction of Geshe Kelsang. The three main Centres are:

Manjushri Centre, Conishead Priory, Ulverston, Cumbria, LA12 9QQ, UK. Tel: 01229-584029. manjushri@tcp.co.uk. Founded 1975.

Madhyamaka Centre, Kilnwick Percy Hall, Pocklington, York, YO4 2UF, UK. Tel: 01759-304832. madhyama@rmplc.co.uk. Founded 1979.

Vajradakini Buddhist Center, 1024 Murl Drive, Irving, Texas 75062-4440, USA. Tel/Fax: 214-570-3091.

Addresses of all the other Centres are available from: James Belither, Secretary, the New Kadampa Tradition (NKT), Conishead Priory, Ulverston, Cumbria, LA12 9QQ, UK. Tel: 01229-584029. kadampa@dircon.co.uk.

Index

The letter 'g' indicates an entry in the glossary.